FEMINISM AND MODERN PHILOSOPHY

D1615691

A feminist approach to the history of modern philosophy reveals new insights into the lives and works of major figures such as Jean Jacques Rousseau and David Hume, and is crucial to an appreciation of the advent of feminist philosophy. *Feminism and Modern Philosophy* introduces students to the main thinkers and themes of modern philosophy from different feminist perspectives, and highlights the role of gender in studying classical philosophical texts.

This book shows how the important figures in the history of modern philosophy have been reinterpreted by feminist theory, including:

- feminist critiques of Descartes's rationalism
- Locke's "state of nature" as it relates to the family
- the charges of misogyny leveled against Kant.

In addition the book introduces lesser-studied texts and interpretations, such as:

- the metaphysics of Leibniz's contemporary, Anne Conway
- Annette Baier's recent presentation and defense of Hume.

Feminism and Modern Philosophy: An Introduction is written in an accessible and lively style, and each chapter ends with a helpful annotated guide to further reading. It will be appropriate for philosophy as well as gender studies courses looking at the development of modern Western thought.

Andrea Nye is Professor Emeritus of Philosophy at the University of Wisconsin–Whitewater. Her recent publications include *Philosophy of Language: The Big Questions* (1998) and *The Princess and the Philosopher: The Letters of Elisabeth of the Palatine to René Descartes* (1999).

UNDERSTANDING FEMINIST PHILOSOPHY
Edited by Linda Martin Alcoff

This major new series is designed for students who have typically completed an introductory course in philosophy and are coming to feminist philosophy for the first time. Each book clearly introduces a core undergraduate subject in philosophy, from a feminist perspective, examining the role gender plays in shaping our understanding of philosophy and related disciplines. Each book offers students an accessible transition to higher-level work on that subject and is clearly written, by an experienced author and teacher, with the beginning student in mind.

GENDER AND AESTHETICS
Carolyn Korsmeyer

FEMINISM AND MODERN PHILOSOPHY
Andrea Nye

FEMINISM AND EPISTEMOLOGY
Phyllis Rooney

FEMINISM AND PHILOSOPHY OF SCIENCE
Elizabeth Potter

FEMINISM AND MODERN PHILOSOPHY

An introduction

Andrea Nye

Routledge
Taylor & Francis Group

NEW YORK AND LONDON

First published 2004
by Routledge
29 West 35th Street, New York, NY 10001

Simultaneously published in the UK
by Routledge
11 New Fetter Lane, London EC4P 4EE

Routledge is an imprint of the Taylor & Francis Group

Typeset in Joanna by The Running Head Limited, Cambridge, UK
Printed and bound in Great Britain by MPG Books Ltd, Bodmin

Library of Congress Cataloging in Publication Data
Nye, Andrea, 1939–
Feminism and modern philosophy : an introduction / Andrea Nye.
p. cm. – (Understanding feminist philosophy)
Includes bibliographical references (p.   ) and index.
1. Philosophy, Modern. 2. Feminist theory. I. Title. II. Series.
B791.N94 2004
190'.82–dc22
2003026264

British Library Cataloguing in Publication Data
A catalogue record for this book is available from the British Library

ISBN 0–415–26654–8 hbk
ISBN 0–415–26655–6 pbk

CONTENTS

Preface: living in time   vii

Introduction: shaping a past   1

1 The virtues of misogyny   12

2 Descartes: man of reason   34

3 John Locke and the state of nature   48

4 Reworking the canon: Anne Conway   64

5 Jean Jacques Rousseau and the noble savage   84

6 David Hume: a friend from the past   99

7 Feminist antinomies: Immanuel Kant   111

8 Feminist critical theory after Kant   127

Afterword: the weight of the past   140

Bibliography of works cited   145
Index   151

PREFACE

Living in time

Humans are temporal beings. Whether you think of time as eternal cycles of recurrence, progress toward an ideal state, decline away from Edenic perfection, or simply unprogrammed change, we know who we are and what we are in time and in relation to time. Without a past—regional, cultural, ethnic, national, familial—we are nobodies, anonymous shifting consciousness without identity or location. Without a future, we are bare subsistences, without intention or purpose.

In contemporary Europe and North America, we leave the material past of our species to sciences like archaeology, evolutionary biology, and anthropology. The study of human ideas, however, is traditionally given to philosophy. How we think (the way we organize our concepts, pattern our reasoning, validate our inferences) and what we think (the principles we take as self-evident, the basic truths we take as given, the ideas we reject as backward and superstitious) are idealized, rationalized, and given a history in philosophy. Philosophy in the present projects back in time the significant steps that led to the current state of our thinking; philosophy in the past foreshadows the successes of the present. As a result, history of philosophy courses can play an important role in university curricula, both in philosophy and in liberal arts programs where they provide part of a required core of general education. "Educated" Westerners, enlightened modern persons not given to religious fanaticism, unscientific spirituality, or prelogical thought, are presumed to know something about the origins of philosophy in ancient Greece. If only dimly aware of medieval thought, they are well versed in the drama of modernism that displaced those "dark ages." They have followed the story of intellectual revolution in the seventeenth and eighteenth centuries. They know about the "Enlightenment" that overthrew the authority of the Catholic Church, drew back the obscuring curtain of dogma and superstition, and established rationality as the standard for all humanity. They have rehearsed critical arguments that cut deeper and deeper into unfounded theological and spiritualist speculation to leave experimental science as the key to knowledge. They know the makers of those arguments. First, the great rationalists of the seventeenth century: Descartes, crusader against archaic Aristotelianism; Spinoza, the persecuted lens grinder with geometric proofs of austere anticlerical pantheism; Leibniz, the statesman, with his logical calculus foreshadowing the age of computers. Then the British: Locke marking out the limits of human knowledge; Berkeley ruling out the material world to sustain his rigorous empiricism; Hume, the skeptic who in the name of reason denied any power to reason. Finally comes the crowning achievement of modernism: the German Kant's masterful fusion of Humean skepticism with rationalist certainty in his *Critique of Pure Reason*.

The excitement of reading these modern masters draws students, men and women, into the field of philosophy. The topics addressed are profound, the reasoning close, the drama of struggle with church censorship and political repression inspirational. No matter one's sex, it seems a grand thing to tear down the antiquated house of medieval knowledge and rebuild it again with Descartes, to map the limits of human understanding with Locke, to take on the contradiction between scientific determinism and moral responsibility with Kant. In the process it is we who take form, not we insignificant animals, but we modern humans, free thinkers whose history culminates in the industrial revolution and the democratic welfare state. The *Treatises* and *Enquiries* of the seventeenth and eighteenth centuries illuminate a "human" understanding, "human" nature, "human" rationality, supposedly shared by all, an ideal for all, a template for Descartes's community of scholars, for Rousseau's liberated republic of free citizens, for Kant's community of ends.

Some of us who were students of philosophy in the 1950s and 1960s paid little attention to the fact that the modern philosophers we studied were all men or that the professors who interpreted their philosophies for us were all men. We tried not to notice the fact that there were very few women among our classmates. Later with the coming of the women's movement the lack of women was harder to ignore. We were aware of the blank stares that would result if we called attention to the masculinity of philosophy. We knew the dismissive questioning that would come if we persisted. Was there any outright misogyny in the reading we were assigned? And even if we were able to find passages in the modern masters that asserted women's inferiority, would not a "rational" person pass over these references as a historical oddity?

Were such passages relevant to responsible philosophical inquiry into the nature of knowledge, morality, or God? Isn't dwelling on the sex of a philosopher reducing philosophy to the level of personal relations or partisan politics?

Nevertheless, women in philosophy were experiencing a growing discomfort. Was this a field we could make our own? Was this our thought that was defined as enlightened modern rationality? Was the history of philosophy our history? We knew the official answer. Yes. Yes, as long as we could keep up with the logic, as long as we could present arguments and debate properly with our male colleagues. Yes. As long as we behaved as professionals, we could be philosophers. Hadn't we heard of Miss Anscombe at Oxford? Or Phillippa Foot. Respected philosophers. And women after all.

The uneasiness persisted. That a few women were respected as philosophers did not do away with the lack of women philosophers in the past. Philosophy is a discipline with a past, established in the past with historical roots, but established apparently by men for men. We had devoted ourselves to a train of thought whose couplings were critical and rational, but also fraternal. The men we studied wrote for and to each other, they met for discussion, they responded to each other's queries. For all their disputes, they were bound together in a common cause. If there were women involved, they played, as far as we could see, supporting roles as patrons, friends, and publicists. If now women were invited to join in the discussion as equals, that did not change philosophy's history. Nor did there appear to be any escape from that history.

Thinking necessarily uses concepts with roots in the past. Always in language, thinking is a reshaping, never an original creation. This is especially true in a text-based tradition such as philosophy. Philosophers are people "of the book." Their Bible is a canon of texts some of which appear on every reading list, texts that define the problems of philosophy. What is philosophy if not Descartes's *Meditations* or Locke's *Treatises*? Without these, it seems, there is no modern philosophy, perhaps no philosophy at all. No matter how warmly we might be welcomed as colleagues in a new liberal age, we women, it seemed, would have to begin philosophizing from men's thoughts. We would come to philosophy as outsiders, subject to an interloper's awkwardness and lack of finesse.

And we were beginning to see that the problem was not just with gender. How can members of any group—faced with a history not their own, a history they did not make, a history from which they have been explicitly and purposefully excluded because of some factor such as class, race, or ethnic origin—how can they make history their own in a way that establishes a viable and non-alienated identity? The problem is compounded when the history is of a tradition as revered as philosophy. An exclusive archaic craft or alchemical science might be expendable, but if the history of philosophy is rejected or disowned, not only are you not a philosopher, you are not a modern, heir to the great revolution in thought that gave birth to science and democratic theory.

Some of the ways feminist philosophers have approached this dilemma are surveyed in the chapters that follow. One obvious first step is a critical rereading of texts. A vast body of feminist critique now exists documenting not just the exclusion of women from the ranks of philosophers, but out-right misogyny and racism expressed in many of the canonical works of the Western tradition. Even when there are no explicit remarks about women, tacit presuppositions of gender and other inequality often support superficially neutral accounts of rationality or justice.

A second, more positive, approach is to find texts by women and other excluded groups to add to the canon. Students may traditionally be assigned only readings by white men; existing texts may include only references to white men; that does not mean that there are no women or no non-white men who might be read as philosophers. Unknown, unpublished, or un-noticed texts can be found to add to the canon, and those additions can alter the way problems in modern philosophy are understood.

A third approach cuts deeper. Is it possible to problematize what are taken as the very conceptual foundations of modern philosophy in the light of critical readings of standard texts, additions to the canon, and contemporary feminist perspectives? Is rationality, the hallmark of modernism, a neutral concept, or covert cover for a European master race determined to domi-nate? Is the "nature of man," defined by modern philosophers like Locke and Hobbes as acquisitive and individualistic, a true universal or the emblem of a small powerful caste of European men? Can any philosophy claim to be universal? Or is the claim to universality and truth itself an illegitimate bid for power?

The dilemma women face as they ask these critical questions is shared by other disadvantaged groups. Modern Western philosophy establishes a stan-dard of civilization—individualistic, entrepreneurial, rational—against an opposition often conceptualized as native, tribal, primitive, underdeveloped, and prelogical, as well as feminine. The history of modern philosophy is

typically told as a story of progress, progress away from feminine senti-
mentality, religious fanaticism, idealist fantasy, and primitive superstition,
progress toward a modern scientific era in which "just" wars are fought effi-
ciently, disease is conquered, and mechanical conveniences ensure the pleasures of life. On the face of it, it would seem self-destructive and atavistic for
any group to disown modernism and the philosophies that are at its heart.
Ancient goddess worship, Afrocentric tribal knowledge, Islamic theocracy,
feminine ethics of care run the danger of relegating non-white, non-male,
or non-European thinkers to the impotent fringes of "alternative" thought,
unable to effect changes in mainstream attitudes and beliefs. On the other
hand, to leave one's own history behind—to leave behind times when
women had power, when there were viable women's communities, or the
uninterrupted history of women's heroic care-giving—to put on the language and manner of philosophy as tradition has defined it, is to lose oneself in the name of an uncomfortable borrowed identity.

Hopefully the dilemma is false. History is not immutable fact, but always
selective, partial, and from the perspective of a changing present moment.
As such it is continually being reshaped. Historical time is not a composite
of fixed atomic moments, but interwoven fabric. A thread pulled at one
place reworks the pattern at another, future or past. Just as Renaissance
scholars worked to bracket a medieval "dark ages" and provide a bridge
between the admired classics of ancient Greece and the emerging sciences of
modern Europe, in the same way feminist historians may succeed in giving
philosophy a different past.

INTRODUCTION

Shaping a past

History has its own history. Narratives that review the way history was written in the past are often prelude to new interpretations of history and new hopes for the future. Semi-mythic legends of the founding of ancient empires, ethnographic surveys for imperial administrators, sacred histories that highlight extraordinary moments of revelation and apocalypse, political chronicles of modern nation states, all have helped successive generations to understand better who they are and what they can hope for. This is true when the historical subject is politics or society, and even more so when the history is of ideas. In the spirit of an objective cataloging of demographic trends or economic data it might be possible to produce descriptions of a society's material life as the continental Annales school of historians attempted after World War II. It might be possible to emulate the natural sciences and apply some version of a covering law to political trends, as C. F. Hempel and Karl Popper proposed in the same era. When the subject is philosophy, it is impossible to avoid interpretation and evaluation. What is to count as philosophy? Which works are included as important? Those considered to be important in their own day? Hardly. Those whose writers had academic status? If so Locke, Hume, and Descartes are off the list. And once the important texts are established, by what principles are they to be interpreted and judged?

As important as the selection of texts and leading ideas is the arranging of those texts and ideas in temporal sequence. A story without a beginning and an end is no story at all. Events have significance in relation to crises and climaxes, initiations and conclusions. Histories of modern philosophy have been noteworthy for a high sense of drama. After a period of darkness—the proverbial "dark ages"—glimmers of "light" show as a first generation of philosopher-scientists in sixteenth-century Europe begin to question, often at their peril, the intellectual authority of the Catholic Church. In the seventeenth century free thinkers like Descartes and Locke spread enlightenment, gradually placing not only natural philosophy but also politics, society, and economics under the sovereignty of reason. In the eighteenth century the fruits of secular rationalism ripen to a grand and positive vision of steady progress, as science projects the coming mastery of disease and hunger, and technology begins to provide the instruments of power by which Western "civilization" will spread to the rest of the world. Steps are taken toward Rousseau's citizen state and Kant's rational "kingdom of ends" in nascent democratic republics in France and America. Ethics breaks loose from hypocritical piety and finds new foundations in natural sentiment, calculated utility, or rational principle. Just as the birth of Jesus provided the focal point for sacred Christian time, Western philosophy divides into before and after. Before is the "premodern" era of Greece, Rome, and medieval Europe. After is the "postmodern" and the hopefully transitory doubts of the present era. In between comes the pivotal miracle of the birth of modernism in the seventeenth and eighteenth centuries.

How to plot the "postmodern" sequel to modernism is still a matter of debate. Sequels, by their very nature, involve not new beginnings but setbacks to be overcome as ways of thought mature and take hold. The period of time from the early 1800s to the two world wars of the twentieth century—a period that is generally covered in the philosophy curriculum under "contemporary philosophy"—saw many such lapses, including the collapse of democracy into Napoleonic authoritarianism, the restoration of ancient monarchies, romantic rebellions against reason and science, idealist and materialist visions that imported providence back into history. As the story is traditionally told, progress in the modern period is too strong to be rescinded. Through temporary regressions to the premodern or primitive, through apocalyptic prophecies of the decline of the West, science continues its steady conquest of the natural world. Political reason continues to make capitalist democracy the norm for "civilized" human society. Philosophy in the second half of the twentieth century, past a Wittgensteinian moment of anxious self-extinction, settles down to the task of ensuring that spiritualism and irrationality do not reinvade a robust scientific realism and "naturalized" epistemology.

The first contemporary feminist qualms about this shaping of history came in the revolutionary fervor of the 1960s. The problem was not so much the fact that major figures in philosophical history were men or that in their writing they used masculine terms. Men can be great thinkers and it might be assumed that, however they were originally meant, expressions like the "nature of man," the rights of "man," "rational man" can now be taken generically. More important was a resurgence of doubt about progress under the banner of modernism. Such doubt was not new. It dates back at least as far as the mid-nineteenth century, when a round of progressive modernist revolutions in Europe failed to keep promises of general well-being. It resurfaced a few decades later, at the turn of the nineteenth century, when European nation states became warring camps vying for territory with all the violence science could devise. Faced with the reality of "world" wars engineered with the naval, manufacturing, and artillery techniques that modern reason makes possible, philosopher-historians like Oswald Spengler traced not the triumphant victory but The Decline of the West. He and his contemporaries saw no progress toward a reconciled and peaceful world. The adventuring, expansionist activities of the West were not part of a grand mission of civilizing and colonizing conversion, but the Faustian excess of a dying empire. The possibility of making universal value judgments gave way among many European historians to skepticism and relativism. The technological and utilitarian ideals of Western culture were on the wane, and it was not clear there was any warrant for extending already compromised values to other cultures. Modern philosophy, closely linked to science and the efficient administration of nation states, was not universal truth, but the ideology of a specific and compromised way of life, rising in a particular geographical space and rapidly coming to the end of its lifespan.

After a second world war and the Holocaust, faith in the ascendancy of the West was further shaken. Emigrant German philosophers like Hannah Arendt interrogated the Western tradition and the "professional philosophers" who had defined it, for some sense of how to go on when tradition has shattered. Tradition, Arendt argued in The Life of the Mind, eases an always anxious transition from the past to the future. It gives necessary assurance, given that any action can turn out to have disastrous results. But when tradition is utterly discredited, as it was in the Holocaust, when its guiding philosophies are put in the service of evil, there is nothing to ease a way forward into the future.

Similar concerns were prominent among American philosophers during and in the aftermath of the Vietnam War. Now it was the new triumphal leader of modernism, the United States, who appeared to be callously slaughtering innocents in the name of reason, progress, and democratic politics. A spokeswoman for these doubts was feminist philosopher Sara Ruddick. In

Maternal Thinking she described her education as a fledgling philosopher in the 1960s. As a student, she read with excitement the great moderns, Descartes, Locke, Kant, along with their heirs—Wittgenstein, Habermas, Peter Winch. When the Vietnam War came and she was involved in the peace and civil rights movements, she began to have doubts. Perhaps philosophic reason, with its abstract concepts and deductive trains of thought, contributed to war by giving the impression that with the right method one could establish truths worth killing for. The fruits of the cognitive revolution of the seventeenth and eighteenth centuries were military and navigational technologies that allowed Europe and now the United States to subjugate non-Western people. In the place of the philosopher's reason with its universal authority, Ruddick proposed a feminine "practicalism," rooted in values, skills, and a sense of reality associated, not with politics or science, but with mothering, an activity that had never been mentioned in her philosophy classes.

Also with roots in the counter-culture of the 1960s was Carolyn Merchant's critical treatment of the origins of modernism in *The Death of Nature*. If an expansionist West asserted itself violently over native "premodern" peoples, Merchant argued, the roots of that assault were in the founding attitude of modernist epistemology that nature is for men to dominate and control. Quoting Francis Bacon, whose defense of reason and independence of thought inspired Descartes and others to challenge Aristotelian science, Merchant explored insistent gender metaphors that shaped the early modern call for the mastery of nature. Nature was a woman to be stripped bare of her veils, penetrated and probed by the masculine hand of science. Her secrets were to be seized from her in heroic feats of experimentation and discovery. It was an insight that the rebels of the counter-culture could take to heart. Not only was the West under the banner of modernist politics crushing native communities in Vietnam and elsewhere, in the name of modernist epistemology and metaphysics it was destroying global environments in ruthless and irresponsible abuse of nature.

Given disillusion with the grand promises of philosophical enlightenment, with nineteenth-century scenarios of idealist or materialist revolution, and with positive visions of material progress, the philosophers who initiated modernism could seem more villains than heroes. Had modernism kept its promise of justice for all? Had poverty been eliminated? Had the ravages of slavery been addressed and repaired? Were women equal to men? Regardless of assertions of progress in implementing modernist goals of equality and liberty, regardless of assurances by Marxists that when private property was abolished women would achieve parity with men, many women philosophers felt the past as oppressive weight. They continued to be a small minority in the field of philosophy. Their work was underrepresented at conferences and in journals. A few feminist critics called attention to misogynous references in the writing of modern philosophers. A few feminist ethicists introduced sexual and gender issues as philosophical problems. But the great canonical body of philosophical writing remained solidly masculine, page after page of dense reasoning that, like it or not, set the agenda for philosophical discussion. The writing of male philosophers was subject to minor critique but not, it seemed, to displacement. In literature—in fiction or essay writing—there were important feminine exemplars, writers who were accepted as part of the literary canon and who were studied in literature classes. Philosophy seemed to have successfully barricaded itself against the female voice.

In the 1980s, new currents of thought from France labeled as "postmodern" or deconstruction directly challenged that barrier and offered new approaches to history. The philosopher's rational subject, argued theorists like Michel Foucault and Jacques Derrida, is a fraud. The projected autonomy of reason—of Descartes's cogito, Locke's natural law, Kant's unity of apperception—is illegitimate and delusory projection and has no substantive reality, any more than does the historian who pretends to tell philosophy's true story. The absolute time that relates and orders events and that is the backbone of conventional history is an invention and an illusion of philosophers. Not only is the time line that prioritizes milestone events a fiction; so is the removed historian who thinks she or he from the vantage of the present can survey and map that sequence objectively.

The skepticism of the new postmodern and deconstructive theorists went deeper than postwar cautions about evidence and hasty generalization. It was not that historians should verify sources, attempt objectively to discover regularities and patterns in data, or be ready to revise their conclusions in the light of new evidence. Instead the reality to which various accounts of historical events could be compared disappeared. What the critic deals with, said the new theorists, is texts, segments of an eternally present world of words from which there is no escape. The distinction between philosophy, the "queen of the sciences," and literature dissolved; philosophy could make no more claim to truth than a novel or a poem. The authority of philosophy as the intellectual backbone of Western superiority was undermined and, along with it, masculine history and masculine pretension.

A popular source among feminists for a postmodern approach to intellectual history was Michel Foucault. Foucault described the difference between traditional and postmodern history in *The Archaeology of Knowledge*. Traditional historians of ideas trace the rise and fall of various ways of thought and their interrelations. They pay attention to temporal sequences, to chronology of publication, to who influenced whom, to the social, institutional events to which writers refer. The new historian, said Foucault, does none of this. He does not look at what "discourses" are about; he looks at internal configurations. He does not trace out a linear development of ideas; he isolates a static set of rules that govern overlapping "epistemes" or modes of thought. He does not study a philosopher's "œuvre" and attempt to guess what he meant by it. His goal is not to discover what a writer "thought, aimed at, experienced, desired" (*Archaeology*, p. 139). He "rewrites"; he "produces a regulated transformation of what has already been written" (p. 140). The relation between the old and the new history, said Foucault, is one of maturity. Interests in who discovered what ideas, or who was influential over whom, are "harmless enough amusements for historians who refuse to grow up" (p. 144). As Foucault condescendingly observed, the more sophisticated postmodern historian "remains unmoved at the moment (a very moving one, I admit) when for the first time someone was sure of some truth" (p. 144).

Foucault's attack on traditional history was attractive to feminists for a number of reasons. First his approach reduced the commanding presence of male philosophers. In his studies of modernism, Foucault rarely discussed philosophers by name. No longer did Locke, Kant, Descartes loom so large. Their thoughts melted away in large discursive regularities not of their or anyone's making. Ideas were not an individual possession or creation but generated in anonymous institutions of power and control. Second, Foucault's archeological or genealogical approach to modernism suggested the possibility of fresh interpretations of oppression. The interrelated epistemes of modernism, said Foucault, were implicated in new and powerful systems of control, control not exercised by police or judges but administered under the auspices of sciences like psychiatry, criminology, and sociology, the very sciences championed by modern philosophers as objective and value-free. Although Foucault's main interest was in the oppression of homosexuality, many feminists saw in his historical studies new ways to understand and subvert the subordination of women.

In the *History of Sexuality*, Foucault claimed to expose the true workings of modernism by mapping out the construction of "sex" as an object in sciences like biology, psychiatry, and criminology. Sex was not a fact to be discovered and researched, but like all objects a result of discursive formations. He showed complex interactions between regimes of knowledge and regimes of power that controlled behavior. In particular feminists were drawn to his graphic descriptions of the ways in which science, backed by philosophical authority, acts on the bodies of deviants, inmates, and patients. Philosophers like Sandra Bartky, Judith Butler, and Jana Sawiki drew on this history to indict the disciplining of women's bodies in beauty regimes, stigmatization of homosexuality, and pornography.

Much of Foucault's historical work was motivated by his own present concern: What were the invisible but powerful forces of repression that misshaped and restricted the lives of homosexuals like himself? Inversion was no longer punished as a crime; for the most part homosexuals were not subject to legalized violence. Nevertheless, they and their "deviant" lifestyle were analyzed, studied, and treated. Women could sympathize. They too were considered "different" and discriminated against. They too had been the victims of research guided by so-called rational principles. Foucault's treatment seemed to hold out hope for a new revolutionary stance in regard to the past. If his studies were often criticized by traditional historians as partial and poorly documented, still he told a story more reassuring than the orthodox story of a steady inexorable march toward rational enlightenment in which women played no role. Epistemes, said Foucault, come and go. Modernism came and will go. A new regime of power may be inevitable. In the meantime, a degree of intellectual freedom can be achieved in the self-conscious mapping of rules and ruptures, and a small amount of material freedom when the authority of the "disciplines" that maintain the rationality of sex and gender difference is undermined and transgressed.

Further transgressive historical techniques were introduced by Jacques Derrida. Drawing on Saussurian structural linguistics, Derrida explained meaning not by reference to objects external to language, but as generated in internal relations between words and constellations of words. The past is present texts that can be plotted and then deconstructed. A student of philosophy does not give an account of what was thought in the past by a particular philosopher, she gives a reading of a text, a creative act of playful association in which her commentator's voice is woven into an existing linguistic fabric. For this purpose, lesser-known writings and minor authors can be more productive of interesting discursive regularities and irregularities than canonical texts. Even in well-known texts, the best-formed concepts

7

can be shown to be ambiguous, the most rigorous proofs to depend on metaphor. Minor asides can be highlighted, bringing down whole edifices of sacrosanct logical argument. Philosophy was no longer distinguishable from literary writing. It too was governed by stylistics and poetics, and without a claim to truth. Inspired by this leveling of the difference between philosophy and literature in which women had always played a role, feminist philosophers found new ways to confront and confound old texts.

Emulating the imaginative and associative commentaries of writers like the French Luce Irigaray, feminists took on the task of deconstructing the philosophic past. In *Speculum de l'autre femme*, Irigaray, a practicing psychoanalyst, chose little-known passages to draw out what she saw as the masculinist illusion of modernity. An obscure passage from Descartes's optics on birthmarks was the pretext for the exposure of the modern subject as mirror image (*Speculum*, pp. 225–37). From a passage in Kant's metaphysics on mirror images, she moved in a deft stream of associations, to modern man's drive to master the natural world. An allusion to Kant's aesthetics led to a meditation on men's metaphorical use and abuse of women and a comparison with the Marquis de Sade (pp. 253–65). Others followed suit. Sarah Kofman psychoanalyzed "Rousseau's Phallocratic Ends" (in Fraser and Bartky (eds), *Revaluing French Feminism*). Michèle Le Dœuff uncovered a metaphorical *Philosophical Imaginary* in Kant's *Critique of Pure Reason*. In the United States. Jane Flax looked for *Thinking Fragments* rather than logical arguments, placing feminist theory squarely in the postmodern camp.

In the new postmodern approaches to history, time itself was suspect, Newtonian absolute time and space were illusions, artifacts of the modernist episteme. The past is what is presently in the past tense; the past is present texts taken as evidence of the past. What is real is language and discursive structures discovered in language. An atemporal approach to philosophy is hardly new. Professors of philosophy with no interest in French literary theory continue to present philosophical ideas in timeless present tense as part of the legacy of modern rationalism. They judge ideas by the logic of the arguments that support them and by the precision of the definitions that establish their meaning. They read historical figures selectively as exemplars of enduring paradigms of thought—Platonism, Cartesianism, utilitarianism, deontological ethics. But behind the scenes in these traditional treatments of philosophical history, an established history of ideas is taken for granted. If the Dutch hermeticist Van Helmont or the German metaphysician Christian Wolff are not read, it is because they do not contribute to a line of analytic thought from British empiricism to Kant. If Plato's *Timaeus* is seldom on the reading list, it is because the mythical ideas presented there no longer have philosophical resonance. If Hume's *Treatise* is read but not his *Essays*, it is because Hume's essays are for a general not a properly academic audience. Postmodern critics took atemporality a step further. Temporal sequences that anchor philosophical practice were leveled, bringing a freedom of materials and themes open to imagination and association. Minor figures could be resurrected; submerged themes could be introduced. Little-read writings and asides could displace major currents of thought.

Some historians, including some feminist historians, condemned the new postmodern treatments of history. What would determine which patterns and structures were really there and not flights of fancy? What would prevent frivolous excursions of thought not grounded in historical evidence? What happened to truth? If there is no reality to what was thought and argued, truth must be relative to a point of view, to the standpoint of whoever writes the history. As a consequence history can be used to serve the purposes of evil as well as good. Nazi historians can chronicle the evil plots of the Jews. Colonial histories can describe the laziness and dishonesty of native peoples. Postmodernism took away the justification for corrective accounts of history, leaving the past dangerously open to political manipulation. The proper corrective to history, some historians argued, is old-fashioned empirical method, the careful examination of documents, and the conservative construction of causal explanation.

Some defenders of orthodoxy were willing to go a cautious step further. Empirical methods alone might not be enough to guarantee that truth is told about the past. Evidence can be selected and slanted for various purposes. In history and in other areas of knowledge, feminists must be on the alert for bias. Marx had argued that bourgeois histories praising modern philosophers' defense of free enterprise and limited government were ideology reflecting the distorted viewpoint of a capitalist ruling class. He argued that the truth about material and intellectual history could be better discovered from a working-class point of view that sees the past more clearly. Drawing and expanding on the Marxist model, some feminist historians proposed a further enlargement of perspective. Men, whether they are capitalists or workers, have motives for ignoring evidence: they will not see the injustice in gender relations; they will not see how gender distorts philosophers' views. Women, on the other hand, with little power, may be in a better position to understand the past.

"Women's history" became a new historical style. Women appeared as historical agents in revised textbooks; chapters were included on mothering or marriage. In philosophy, women historians began to investigate ways in which assumptions about gender shaped and misshaped theories of justice or knowledge. The unsettled state of thinking about the meaning of history and the proper approach to the history of philosophy energized feminist philosophy. At stake was more than women's unjust exclusion in any historical period, and more than the discovery of historical sources for a present wave of feminist activism. These would continue to be important concerns of feminist philosophers, as work proceeded on women's lives and gender relations in the seventeenth and eighteenth centuries. There was also a deeper question. Is there an objective space in which events can be located? Is there a linear time line on which the causal relations between events and ideas can be traced? Is the vantage point of the present from which the past is viewed a contingent facet of human consciousness that can be overcome or a necessary constituent of reality as it is experienced by human beings? Can feminist historians or any historians steer a safe course between self-serving wishful thinking and false universality? In a new era of self-questioning, feminists looked for a proper balance between an individual's thoughts and the social and political context within which and about which she or he thinks, between thinkers' consciously intended positions and their unconscious assumptions and motives.

Such questions had been debated by Western historians in one form or another for centuries, but had less play in the history of philosophy. Political and social events might be viewed from different perspectives and be open to interpretation. Philosophy, on the other hand, often made the claim to be a realm of pure ideas, existing independently of social context, politics, or gender. Modern philosophy, if well founded and cogently argued, was supposed to be timeless, true of women as well as men, Africans as well as whites, Asians as well as Europeans. Once wrong turns, blind alleys, and gross fallacies were identified and corrected, philosophy could appear as a logical sequence of thoughts from the early modern period to the present day. Possible bias was a defect in reasoning to be corrected by attention to logic. In feminist approaches to philosophy that independence from distorting perspective was eroding.

As outsiders to the shaping of philosophy, women were naturally skeptical about its assumptions. Barred from unthinking adherence to current philosophical practice, they approached its history with new questions. How had modern philosophy evolved? What was the genesis of modern philosophy's perennial problems? What might be the sequel to modern philosophy in an age of disillusion and skepticism? If the concepts that philosophers used in their arguments harbored attitudes and connotations that cannot be understood without reference to relations between men and women, could the history that produced those attitudes and connotations be reshaped?

Further reading

Popular contemporary histories of the legacy of modern philosophy range from the optimism of F. Fukuyama's *The End of History and the Last Man* to the indictments of modernist reason in Richard Rorty's *Philosophy and the Mirror of Nature* and Alaisdair MacIntyre's *After Virtue*. For an overview of feminist appropriations of Rorty's and Foucault's view of history, as well as a discussion of other feminist approaches to historiography, see "Feminism in History of Philosophy" by Genevieve Lloyd in *The Cambridge Companion to Feminism in Philosophy* edited by Miranda Fricker and Jennifer Hornsby.

Elisabeth Ermath's *Sequel to History: Postmodernism and the Crisis of Representational Time* is a good source for a postmodern view of history. For doubts about postmodern history see *Telling the Truth about History* by Joyce Appleby, Lynn Hunt, and Margaret Jacob. A variety of philosophical reactions to postmodernism can be found in Linda Nicholson's collection, *Feminism/Postmodernism*. Various views of the value of French feminist thought are included in Nancy Fraser and Sandra Bartky's collection of essays, *Revaluing French Feminism*. Time from a postmodern perspective is the subject of a collection edited by John Bender and David Wellbery, *Chronotypes: The Construction of Time*.

A range of views on Foucault's importance for feminists can be found in *Feminist Interpretations of Michel Foucault*, edited by Susan Hekman, and in *Feminism and Foucault: Reflections on Resistance*, edited by Irene Diamond and Lee Quinby. The Hekman volume is one in a series of collections of feminist essays on major philosophers, including also Hume and Kant, under the general editorship of Nancy Tuana. Tuana's introduction in each of the volumes gives an overview of problems and issues that motivate feminist work in the history of philosophy.

1

THE VIRTUES OF MISOGYNY

Feminine traits are called weaknesses. People joke about them; fools ridicule them; but reasonable persons see very well that those traits are just the tools for the management of men, and for the use of men for female designs.

Immanuel Kant, *Anthropology*, p. 217

The quest for abstract and speculative truths, principles, and axioms in the sciences, for everything that tends to generalize ideas, is not within the competence of women . . . Nor do women have sufficient precision and attention to succeed at the exact sciences. Woman, who is weak and who sees nothing outside the house, estimates and judges the forces she can put to work to make up for her weakness, and those forces are men's passions.

Jean Jacques Rousseau, *Emile*, pp. 386–7

As nature has given *man* the superiority over *woman*, by endowing him with greater strength, both of mind and body; it is his part to alleviate that superiority, as much as possible, by the generosity of his behavior, and by a studied deference and complaisance for all her inclinations and opinions.

David Hume, *Essays*, p. 133

In post-World War II Britain and North America, with the analytic paradigm for philosophy in full sway, philosophers' views on women were seldom a subject of discussion. Kant's *Anthropology* was considered peripheral, unrelated to core issues in modern philosophy—the resolution of skeptical doubt, the discrediting of dogmatic theology, and reconciliation of naturalistic determinism and free will. Kant's views on sexuality and women, when they were mentioned at all, were dismissed as personal idiosyncrasy or due to prejudices of his times. Kant himself could be cited in support. In the introduction to the 1785 *Foundations of the Metaphysics of Morals*, he announced his aim to construct a moral philosophy independent of anthropology. Women, contemplating Kantian ethics—an ethics that denies the importance of feeling or passion—could find Kant's resolve to steer clear of human nature puzzling. What is this "anthropology" that is to be left behind if a man is to be moral?

Man in his physical existence, Kant explained in his *Anthropology*, is a poor creature. Driven by lust, jealousy, and greed, he is worse than an animal whose behavior has regularity enforced by natural instinct. Man's freedom from the constraints of instinct means that passion can lay hold of him, impose on him a necessity before which all other demands must give way. At the same time freedom from instinct is man's escape from passion and his one redeeming feature. Man can, if he chooses, reason and freely will what reason commands. What distinguishes man as a species, Kant wrote, is that man is a "reasonable being endowed with freedom" (*Anthropology*, p. 195). He has the capability to act by pure force of will, but according to the requirements of reason and not passion.

Kant's *Anthropology* was published at the end of his life, but his thoughts on the nature of man and woman had been a long time developing. Early on he had discovered and thrilled to Rousseau's discussion of natural man and woman in *Emile*. In passionate detail Rousseau described the education that would allow man's true nature to flower. He described the woman who would be the ideal mate for natural man. Kant read David Hume's *Essays* in which Hume commented on femininity and on relations between the sexes. Like many of the moderns, Kant was a reader of travel books, familiar with Captain Cook's adventures on South Sea islands with beautiful willing native women, Indian braves decorated for mating dances with beads and feathers, strange practices of polygamy and wife-trading. Never did he let go, said Kant, of the insight that struck him when first reading Rousseau. Understanding the human nature of man is the necessary foundation for ethics even if it is that very nature that moral man must transcend.

Kant described such moral transcendence in the *Anthropology*. The ability to deny passion and to act from rationally determined dispassionate will is not given by nature. A man is not born with it. It must be acquired in a kind of "rebirth." In midlife, around the age of forty, a man—a man like himself—may undergo a crisis. At this point, there can be "an explosion which suddenly occurs as a consequence of our disgust at the unsteady condition of instinct" (*Anthropology*, p. 206). The result can be utter cynicism, debauchery, or despair, but the crisis can also lead to a dramatic conversion. A resolve or decision can be made in which a man becomes a man of "character," capable of resisting passion and objects that arouse passion. Although this change in a man has minimal requirements of rationality and can be achieved by the "ordinary human mind," there are many for whom it is difficult or impossible. Poets, clergymen, and courtiers have too much invested in pleasing their masters to achieve moral character. Women are completely disqualified.

Women, said Kant, have principles, but these principles are "hard to relate with character in the narrow sense of the word" (*Anthropology*, p. 222). They have character, but in the sense that a natural kind has character. They have principles, but these are the result not of autonomous reasoning but of maxims like "what is generally believed is true" or "what people generally do is good." Misogynous anecdotes were readily available. Did not the poet Milton's wife urge him out of social ambition to join Cromwell's government, a government he had previously called illegal? Did not the proverbially shrewish wife of Socrates mar the high tone of the great philosopher's deathbed by breaking in to complain of the destitute state in which he left her and their children? Of course, Milton and Socrates, being men of character, were not deterred from acting on "principle." He can say this, quipped Kant, without diminishing the credit due to the feminine "character." Women have a character, a character given by nature, a character ordained by biology.

If the reason why clergymen and courtiers cannot achieve full humanity and moral maturity is social, owing to the deference these functionaries must pay to church officials, ruling monarchs, and mistresses, the reason why women cannot achieve moral maturity is "nature's design." Nature requires, Kant explained, that the species propagate. For that purpose union between men and women is necessary, a union in which difference is needed to ensure a cohesive fit. For such a union to be stable "one person must subject himself to the other, and, alternately one must be superior to the other in something so he can dominate or rule" (*Anthropology*, p. 216). If man and woman are identical there will be conflict. Nature's solution is to make men superior in reason, strength, and courage, and to give women a compensatory power to say no to men's sexual desires. If women were totally lacking in power, men would rule like brutes, which they in fact do in "uncivilized countries" where the woman's power of denial is not fully developed and the man's strength is unchallenged. In "savage" lands, confidently reports Kant, men rule with clubs and women do all the work. In civilized countries a man's superior power is kept in check by a woman's ability to deny him sex until he accedes to what she wants. What she wants is the protection of marriage. Nature makes women alluring and gives them power over men, "so that [men] would find themselves imperceptibly fettered by a child due to their own magnanimity" (p. 219).

People make fun of a woman's loquacity, timidity, quarrelsomeness, and childishness, but, said Kant, these traits are no joke. They are the key to a woman's power. They allow her to attract and entice men and then hold out for marriage. In that way a woman ensures not only procreation but support for herself and her children. At the height of "civilization" in European society, even married women, Kant reported disapprovingly, are allowed to flirt so as to have a ready stock of husbands in reserve in case they lose or desert their present mates. After marriage woman's primary drive is to dominate men and eliminate other women as rivals; this is all part of "nature's design" so that the species is propagated. A woman's virtues are consistent with her natural design. A man's virtue is to be tolerant, perceptive, and jealous of his wife; a woman's virtue is to be patient, sensitive, and jealous of every other woman (*Anthropology*, pp. 221–2). A woman *reigns* in "civilized" marriages as a frivolous spendthrift monarch; a proper husband *rules* as a sober prime minister.

Women are not suited to be intellectual companions. Here Kant echoed the educational policies of his hero Rousseau. "As for scholarly women," said Kant, "they use their books somewhat like a watch, that is, they wear the watch so it can be noticed that they have it on, although it is usually broken or does not show the time" (*Anthropology*, p. 221). Certainly Kant did not contemplate that women would participate in the modern enlightenment that he considered to be the great achievement of his age. If Kant noted the reluctance of many men to be released from self-incurred tutelage and think for themselves, he reported the total refusal of women. "The step to competence is held to be very dangerous by the far greater portion of mankind (and by the entire fair sex)" ("What Is Enlightenment?" in *On History*, p. 3).

After extended remarks on women's nature in the *Anthropology*, Kant has a

moment of self-consciousness. Has he "dwelt longer on the subject of characterization [of the sexes] than seems proportionate to other divisions of
anthropology?" But, he explains, there is an important "pragmatic" point to
be made. One must appreciate the "wisdom of nature's gradually unfolding
designs" (*Anthropology*, p. 225). Consorting with women is a necessary evil, at
least for some men, so that the species continue. If possible, however, it is
better to avoid close contact with women. And Kant followed his own advice.
After an early tentative interest, he disavowed marriage and, it would seem,
carnal attachment of any kind. By the final statement of his ethics in the *Metaphysics of Morals*, sex has become a source of degradation. Even under the best
of circumstances in marriage, where the sexual use of another is exclusive
and mutual by contract, sex without the practical aim of procreation is
morally compromising.

These and other misogynous remarks make Kant an obvious target for
feminist critics. Feminist philosophers cited Kant's prudish disgust at a
woman's body, his contempt for women's intelligence and ethical capability,
his defense of a "patriarchal" law of marriage in which a woman has no
legal rights. They pointed out the obvious contradiction between Kant's
views on women and the moral principle that human beings are to be
treated as ends not means. They condemned his relegation of women to a
biological function.

But why not lay aside Kant's misogyny as an aberration unworthy of serious notice? This was the view of many readers of Kant, including the editor
of the 1978 edition of the *Anthropology*, Frederick Van de Pitte. Van de Pitte was
no conservative in questions of philosophical content. He noted with
approval that by the late 1970s what was considered proper philosophical
subject matter had expanded. Ideas from the continent, from thinkers like
Martin Heidegger and Ernst Cassirer, were back in fashion. There was movement away from an overemphasis in English-speaking philosophy on logical
analysis and epistemology. If Kant's *Anthropology* seems peculiar to English-
speaking readers, commented Van de Pitte, it is because "the English-speaking
world has too long restricted its consideration to a purely empirical anthropology." European thinkers on the other hand kept alive the "notion of a
genuinely philosophical anthropology" (*Anthropology*, p. xxi). In that spirit
Kant's work on the nature of man is essential, claimed Van de Pitte, if commentators are to understand the purpose of Kant's philosophy and the degree
to which it is prescriptive rather than narrowly descriptive.

But even the liberal Van de Pitte denied the philosophical importance of

Kant's comments on women. The *Anthropology* gives us insight into Kant the man, he said. It shows us Kant's wide reading, his interest in travel literature, his use of explorers' tales to prove generalizations about human nature. The *Anthropology* is proof of Kant's taste and his concern for the social graces. If it also exhibits some lapses from good will, these should be set aside. Important though personal qualities may be from a biographical point of view, "from the philosophical standpoint, information about Kant as an individual is the least interesting aspect of the *Anthropology*" (p. xx). On that ground, Van de Pitte had no trouble dismissing what he called Kant's rather "amazing" views on women and non-white races: "Kant *was* a man of goodwill," he stated categorically, "and any failure on his part to live up to the moral ideal must be ascribed to a lack of experience which permitted his prejudices to remain undetected" (p. xx).

In fact, Kant did have experience with women. Throughout his life, he was a frequent guest at aristocratic households where he learned to ingratiate himself with fashionable hostesses. He moved in freewheeling literary circles where boisterous partying and sexual intrigue were common. As a young man he had several romantic adventures. Long sections on women in his early *Observations on the Feeling of the Beautiful and Sublime* show him preoccupied with women and not always in a derogatory sense. The young Kant, not yet a man of character, may have been bashful and uncomfortable in the presence of women, but judging from his "observations" on feminine beauty, he was also romantically taken by them.

Kant's subject in the *Observations* is aesthetics in the wider sense popularized in England by Shaftesbury and in Germany by Baumgarten. Aesthetics in this sense is not the study of classical rules of genre, but the exploration of pleasurable response to all sorts of phenomena, in nature, decorative arts, architecture, persons. In this early work, unlike the later *Critique of Pure Reason* in which reason is the same for all men, Kant embraces diversity as a positive factor and a rich source for discoveries about beauty (*Observations*, p. 45). Continually he notes the personal nature of his "observations" as he explores varied and complex reactions to objects, including passionate and romantic responses to feminine beauty. Women for this younger Kant are the beautiful sex and his description of their distinctive character and worth is in many places a poetic hymn of praise to the charming "difference" of feminine grace and amiability.

Women are kind-hearted and responsive. Male passions at best spur a man on to his moral duty and at worst make him a monster. Women's feelings are sensitive and accurate so women can act benevolently without the compulsion of duty. In moral matters, women do not need to act on principle; they can "broaden" and enlarge their feelings, cultivating a form of direct moral response. Even vanity, a vice in a man, can make a woman more beautiful if she uses her beauty to soften and attract. A woman's nobility is of a different kind from a man's, said Kant. She is noble in her modesty, simplicity, benevolence, her respect for others, and her trust in herself. Her noble qualities survive aging when moral beauty rather than purely physical beauty shines through. Even passages where Kant deprecates women's intellectual ability can be read as a kind of praise. A woman, says Kant, has no need of academic erudition, which requires painful effort and can mar her beauty. She need know only enough about Leibniz's monads or Descartes's vortices to see the joke when such abstruse constructions are satirized at dinner parties.

In this early work, far from being the moral downfall of man, feeling, especially feminine feeling, is a possible source of moral insight. Already Kant has doubts about personal sentiment as a basis for morality, but instead of denying sentiment a role in morality as he does later, here he elaborates on what can give sentiment moral force. Women provide his examples. Sympathy and sociability, he argues, can be broadened, can be made a kind of principle so that morality is stabilized. Principle here is not the categorical imperative of the later *Critiques*, nor is it Hume's calculation of utility. A broadening of sentiment, Kant says, is due not to "speculative rules" but to a "feeling" for "the beauty and dignity of human nature" that expands and extends impulses of sympathy and sociability (*Observations*, p. 60). Feeling in a woman is not ancillary or "adoptive"; her kindheartedness is broad enough so that she does not need to think in terms of duty, does not need to be subjected to laws that govern her behavior. Not only are women able to broaden their feeling in this way, they can awaken such enlarged feelings in men. If impulse and inclination were all, a man would lose interest in his wife when she ages. A broadened appreciation for her keeps love alive. A desire for honor, for the favorable judgment of others, provides an impulse to "take a standpoint outside himself in thought, in order to judge the outward propriety of his behavior as it seems in the eyes of the onlooker" (p. 75).

If the Kant of the *Observations* has doubts about women they are liberally spiced with romance. Kant, whose health, at least in his own mind, was fragile, expressed worries about the sex act, but never the disgust and loathing of his later *Metaphysics of Morals*. On to sexual desire "the finest and liveliest inclinations of human nature are grafted" (*Observations*, p. 84).

18

The European alone has found the secret of decorating with so many flowers the sensual charm of a mighty inclination and of interlacing it with so much morality that he has not only completely elevated its agreeableness but also has made it very decorous.

(p. 112)

To preserve these finer feelings and to guard against disgust, a certain reticence and shame are necessary, but a purely physical appreciation of a woman's looks is not to be disdained, especially if added to it is a taste for moral beauty, for a face that indicates a benevolent heart and inner feeling that will last past youth.

Even here there is a note of disillusion. The common man with simple straightforward, if crude desires may be better off than a romantic, wrote Kant. A common man's simple physical feelings are easily satisfied. He can go on to devote his attention to practical matters such as creating a household and handling money matters. For the man of finer feeling, the man of refined aesthetic taste, a man like himself, romance is more difficult. Reticence can cool his "impetuous ardor"; he is often disappointed when a woman fails to live up to his expectations, or worse, when she passes him over and chooses a seducer or a fop. Such a man may hesitate when contemplating marriage as a young man. He may postpone or even abandon marriage. If he rushes into commitment he may be racked with peevish regret that he made the wrong choice. Romance for this man of finer taste is often tragic romance, romance seldom consummated except in his imagination, because he holds on to the idea that marriage is a sacred union, creating a "single moral person" (*Observations*, p. 95). Marriage for this man must be a perfect match between a man's understanding and a woman's sensitivity, in which both husband and wife are inclined only to please the other so there is never any conflict, never any question of man's *right* to rule or woman's *duty* to obey. Even under these ideal circumstances, there is work involved: a man must struggle to keep sexual desire alive so as to perform his marital duty and realize the great natural purpose of marriage.

Many years later, in the *Anthropology*, descriptions surface that recall this youthful romanticism, but in a darker light. Again Kant describes a young man's nervous advances to women.

Early in life, the woman acquires confidence in her ability to please. The young man always manages to displease and, consequently, is

19

embarrassed (feels awkward) in the company of ladies. By virtue of her sex, she maintains a feminine haughtiness in order to restrain all importunities of men through the respect, which haughtiness instills; and she claims the privilege of respect even without deserving it. The woman is unwilling; the man is insistent; her yielding is a favor.

(*Anthropology*, p. 220)

In retrospect, the romantic made a fool of himself. His worshipful feelings were ridiculous. The women he approached were worldly, hardly interested in an inexperienced and awkward youth no matter how appreciative he is of them.

In another passage, Kant compared a young man's naïve and bumbling approach to a pretty "girl" to a rustic peasant traveling to the city for the first time. Like the peasant who has to ask directions, the unsophisticated suitor receives from the knowing woman a "benevolent smile." Her smile expresses "good-natured and kindly ridicule at inexperience," a good-natured tolerance "based on the evil art of pretense, indicative of our already corrupted human nature" (*Anthropology*, p. 16). The innocent newcomer to fashionable flirtation is a joke for sexual adventurers and worldly seductresses. As the poor youth languishes, other men, Kant observes, men who are less scrupulous and less innocent, are busy pretending to be gallant while all the time they only strive to satisfy crude physical desire. "How much cleverness has been wasted in throwing a delicate veil over man's desires, but revealing still enough of man's close relation to the animal kingdom so that bashfulness results" (p. 20).

Kant found little in his reading of modern philosophy to change his mature convictions about women's unreliability. Rousseau, whom he read with enthusiasm, was the popular expert on women's education. The crucially different nature of women demands different treatment, explained Rousseau in *Emile* and other writings. Women are made for man, made to bear a man's children, made to attract and please man, made to ensure that a man cares for his children as his own. Rousseau described the façade of weakness and modesty that in his view was necessary to restrain and contain the dangerous manipulative power of women to excite men's desires. Women play with men, pretend to be weak, use wiles and ruses, stage scenes in which they are overcome by force, wield the "modesty and shame with which nature armed the weak in order to enslave the strong" (*Emile*, p. 358).

20

With the rhetorical flourish that made him popular reading among both men and women, Rousseau warned of the danger if women were not properly trained in restraint and modesty. "Given the ease with which women rouse men's senses and reawaken in the depths of their hearts the remains of ardors which are almost extinguished, men would finally be their victims and would see themselves dragged to death without ever being about to defend themselves" (p. 359). Women "sharpen at their leisure the weapons with which they subjugate us" (p. 363).

Many of Kant's expressions in the *Anthropology* recall Rousseau's dramatic warnings of men become women's puppets, men used and exhausted physically, men tormented by doubt about their children's paternity, men driven to their death by an insatiable woman's demands. In Rousseau Kant found support for his claim that women should not undertake philosophy, science, or any abstract rational thought. Women's education should be true to their "nature" and their "natural function" as mothers and wives; it should make them good, dutiful, and obedient. Properly educated in moral restraint, chastity, and the decorative arts, women would produce healthy children and provide for men intimate refuge from the rigors and loneliness of public life.

Kant did read the calmer and more urbane David Hume, who at times seemed to champion the "ladies." In one essay cited by Kant, Hume chided men as well as women (Hume, "On Love and Marriage" in *Essays*, pp. 557–62; cited by Kant, *Anthropology*, p. 223). Hume asked, why do women take offense whenever men speak against marriage? Is this a tacit admission that marriage is a benefit only to women? Is it an expression of guilty conscience that women are to blame when marriages fail? He would like very much to write a hymn of praise to marriage, Hume quipped, but observing what goes on around him it would have to be a satire. The ladies would not want him to misrepresent the facts, would they? But in case men were laughing too loudly at women's expense, Hume turned the question on them. Why is it that men are so against marriage? Because of women's desire to dominate, a desire that takes precedence even over their vanity? But why should men be so worried about a woman's domination if in fact men are the stronger sex? Can it be that men have a bad conscience because they often tyrannize over women and abuse their superior strength? Why, Hume laments, should there have been such a destabilizing difference in strength between men and women, so that from the beginning relations between the sexes are unbalanced?

21

Hume's solution fell short of Kant's sacred ideal of perfect union. A man can fall in love for pleasure, said the practical Hume. He can marry for home, children, and security. If he chooses a mate who gives both sexual pleasure and security the marriage may be relatively happy. In contrast to Kant's conservative insistence on monogamous legal marriage, Hume was a liberal in sexual matters. A woman should be allowed to choose her husband, or at least veto a husband she cannot love. In taking this stand, Hume placed himself with enlightened bourgeois and aristocratic families who were questioning whether a daughter should be made to marry against her will for property and position. Women in the sophisticated circles in Paris and London frequented by Hume met prospective mates in mixed company and expressed preference in husbands. If those husbands allowed their wives to mingle with men in the salons, even form romantic attachments when the ardor of marriage had cooled, it left the men free to do the same. Hume himself profited from such freedoms, especially in Paris where the most absorbing of many love affairs blossomed with the beautiful Comtesse de Boufflers.

In "Of Polygamy and Divorce", Hume defended utility not duty as the standard by which to judge marital arrangements (*Essays*, pp. 181–90). Also a reader of journals of the Cook voyages, he cited the possible utility of temporary marriages between sailors and Polynesian girls in the South Seas, as well as polygamy and divorce on demand. With a degree of irony, he played with his readers' orientalist fantasies. Take harems in Asiatic countries. Given "that slavery to the females, which the natural violence of our passions has imposed on us," such an arrangement can be useful for a man. If he has many wives, he is no longer beholden to one for sex but can play off one wife against another and rule by "mutual jealousy." Even though there is a tyrant ruling over him in some distant provincial capital, at home he is the absolute master of many. But do not judge utility too quickly, said the skeptical Hume. Would European men really want such relationships? Would they want to give up being loved in favor of an absolute rule over a harem of wives? Would they want to give up the pleasures of courtship? Would they want to live so that families could not visit together, so that a man's women had to be kept sequestered under lock and key? Would they want their children to be brought up by slaves? "Destroy love and friendship, what remains in the world worth accepting?" (p. 171). Perhaps European-style monogamy is best after all for men as well as women, especially when you add the possibility of divorce in extreme cases along with the expectation that husband

and wife will eventually settle down to being friends with common interests after romance cools and perhaps even find discreet romance elsewhere.

Some feminists found support for feminist resistance in these and other passages. In an essay "On Moral Prejudice" Hume used the example of a liberated woman to illustrate "moral prejudice." He acknowledged the legitimacy of women's complaints about men's tyranny, inconstancy, jealousy, and indifference (*Essays*, pp. 538–44). He asked his readers to imagine a woman who decides to live alone, to make her own way, not content to endure an abusive husband or even to "share" a man's privileges. What if she goes even further and decides to conceive and raise a child out of wedlock? She will be condemned by public opinion, but that condemnation, concluded Hume, reflects "moral prejudice."

In *An Inquiry concerning the Principles of Morals*, supporting his thesis that principles of justice and rights have their origin in "convenience," Hume used animals, native peoples, and women as examples. If there is no justice due to animals, it is because animals are totally without power to defend themselves against humans or to make their resentments known or felt. As a result there is no utility in extending the doctrine of rights to include animals. The same may be true, said Hume, of races so primitive as to be totally without power, and of women in uncivilized parts of the world. But in Europe women have achieved a different status; they are not like "savages" or animals. Men have the physical power in all countries to enslave women, but in civilized nations "such are the insinuation, address, and charms of their fair companions, that women are commonly able to break the confederacy and share with the other sex in all the rights and privileges" (*Inquiry*, III, I, pp. 21–2).

Hume's tone when speaking of women is free of Rousseau's panic and Kant's bitterness, but much of the substance of what he says about women is equally demeaning. Women are different from men. Women are modest and retiring; they do not risk themselves; they do not put themselves forward as men do. Women are not suited to rigorous study. He recommends only light history for the "ladies," and responding to imagined female protest, he is affectionately condescending, playfully confessing that he has been "seduced with a kind of raillery against the ladies." Perhaps they will forgive him and understand that this kind of joking attention "proceeds from the same cause which makes the person who is the favorite of the company to be often the object of their good-natured jests and pleasantries." Can he not "presume that nothing will be taken amiss by a person who is secure of the good opinion and affection of everyone present?" He will be more serious, he promises, adopting the tone one might take to a pretty child. He will point out the advantages of reading history for "those debarred from the severer studies by the tenderness of their [constitution] and the weakness of their education" (*Essays*, p. 565). In the end, Hume does not protest the educational policies of his friend Rousseau. If education and convention enforce reticence and chastity for women instead of natural design, nowhere does Hume hold out hope that it should be any other way. If European women manage to win a "share" of European men's prerogative, it will be, just as Kant will later reiterate in more hostile terms, by charm and insinuation rather than by an exercise of power in their own right.

Hume's explanation for women's reticence is different from Kant's but no more to a woman's credit. For the mature Kant, modesty is a cunning "design" of nature so that women can manipulate men and achieve the reproduction of the species. For Hume, the ideal of chastity comes from utility, "from education, from the voluntary conventions of men, and from the interest of society" (*Treatise of Human Nature*, III, II, xii, p. 621). The root cause is not biology but a response by society to the biological fact that reproduction requires a man and a woman to remain together so that men can support and protect women and children. The explanation is different but the effect is the same. For men to agree to "this restraint, and to undergo chearfully all the fatigues and expenses to which it subjects them," they need to be sure that children are theirs. Given the power of the sexual urge in women as well as men, internalized feelings of shame and modesty are the effective way to restrain women's sexual activity. To deter women from the always powerful temptation of sex, they must be trained from childhood to suppress their sexuality. The gallant respect that Hume recommends to "alleviate" masculine superiority cedes even less power to women, it might be argued, than Kant's fearful resentment. Given the social utility Hume sees in controlling women's fertility, there is no real prospect for women's independence. They can share the prerogatives of husbands, they can win some consideration as wives and mothers, but not much more.

There were other philosophers Kant could have read, Mary Wollstonecraft, for example. The education Rousseau prescribed for women, Wollstonecraft wrote in *A Vindication of the Rights of Woman*, reflects a general decline in French morality. It is an education that is bound to produce not morality but the very libertinism, sentimentalized pornography, duplicitous lust, corrupt manners, and immodesty in women and men that Rousseau deplored. Rational thought, argued Wollstonecraft, is the only solid basis for morals, whether the morals of men or women. Instead Rousseau would educate women to be sex objects and slaves, with all the defects in morality that accompany these conditions.

Wollstonecraft was first in a long line of feminist critics to analyze psychologically what she saw as deformations in male character that distort men's thinking. Rousseau's "errors in reasoning arose from sensibility," she said (Vindication, p. 197). As a youth, an overwhelming ambivalent emotional response to women resulted in unhealthy lascivious fantasies. "When he should have reasoned he became impassioned, and reflection inflamed his imagination instead of enlightening his understanding," diagnosed Wollstonecraft (p. 197). Rousseau was born with a "warm constitution and a lively fancy," very much attracted to the opposite sex. If he had been able to give way to those feelings in a healthy way his passions would have moderated. Instead a warped sense of virtue and sickly romantic prudery prevented the normal outlet for his feelings. Once repressed, sexual impulse had to find expression in either debauched imaginations or a frenzied froth of romantic sylvan bliss.

Kant did not read Wollstonecraft, and it is unlikely that he would have been able to see much of himself in her analysis of male attitudes if he had. As far as he was concerned, he had avoided passion; he had not romanticized marriage; he had seen the sex act for what it was, a selfish and morally compromised use of another's body. He had his "rebirth" and became a mature man of character. He recognized passion as a cancer, "an illness that abhors all medication" (Anthropology, pp. 172–3). In his Lectures on Ethics, he taught a moral duty to self, to a man's dignity and independence. He taught self-respect based on freedom from passion, sex, and women's power as "the supreme condition and the principle of all morality" (Lectures, p. 121). Even if a man mistreats others, if he does not dishonor his own person sexually in fornication or masturbation he has moral worth. It is dishonor not to be in full control of one's feelings. It is degrading to give in to drunkenness, servility, lying, accepting favors, grief, and most important lust. To submit to sexual desire is to "abandon ourselves to others in order to satisfy their desires," to make oneself an object of enjoyment. Masturbation, homosexuality, prostitution, keeping a mistress are "loathsome," "gross," worse even than suicide as moral faults. Even in fantasy they must be repressed and the body maintained as moral duty.

Women's old power for Kant has not disappeared; what has disappeared is its power to charm. Women are no longer in need of gallantry or protection. They are a dangerous force, able to exercise tyranny over men. In the

Anthropology even women's inferior legal status is evidence of their power. Women, said Kant, have so "glib" a tongue, they hardly need anyone to defend them in court. In this regard, a woman is "more than of age" and can ably defend both herself and her husband. Having unjustly achieved the status of weaker sex in public, women have more power at home in compensation. A woman's status as legal minor may be degrading; it is also "comfortable." She can be an autocrat in the house and subject her husband to "permanent tutelage" (*Anthropology*, p. 106).

It is impossible to know for certain what caused the change in tone between the romance of the *Observations* and the harsh moralism of Kant's *Lectures on Ethics*. A logician might give a simple answer. Kant saw a fallacy in basing morality on feeling. Wollstonecraft might cite the influence of psychological complexes dating from a rigid and repressed pietist upbringing. But one particular incident in Kant's life seems to have been a turning point. As a young man, Kant contemplated marriage. On one occasion, he waited too long and like the cautious disappointed suitor in the *Observations* was rejected. He had several other glancing relationships. Then came a situation that gave him much pain.

Before and during the period he wrote the *Observations* Kant was on close terms with a literary couple, Johann Jacobi and his lively, attractive, and much younger wife, Maria Charlotta. Kant had been a friend of Johann for some time, but with the wife he was on more intimate terms judging from at least one flirtatious and suggestive letter. Tiring of her inattentive older husband, Maria Charlotta cultivated other relationships, including a flirtation with Kant, himself considerably older at thirty-eight. As the cautious Kant dallied or more likely demurred, Maria Charlotta turned her attention elsewhere. She fell in love with a mutual friend, took the friend as lover, resourcefully got herself a divorce, and remarried. Kant was racked with conflicting emotions, jealousy, regret, chagrin, and anger. With friends laughing at him behind his back, he made himself ridiculous. He loudly expressed outrage at the marriage, said nasty things to Johann about his former wife, refused to go to the wedding or to see the new couple, all of which gave rise to much gossip and joking at his expense. After this humiliating incident, chastened by the frank and self-assertive behavior of Marie Charlotte, Kant ruled out marriage. His view of women hardened. Further embittered by the death of a friend and increasing evidence that women were on occasion unfaithful to husbands, Kant began his crisis of character. Ten "silent" years later emerged the critical rationalist of philosophical history.

Interesting biography. But what does frustrated romance or sophisticated dalliance in Parisian salons have to do with philosophy? What do romantic troubles have to do with the skeptical doubts that jolt a man out of dogmatic slumber and lead him to construct a critical metaphysics? What do personal attitudes have to do with core issues in ethics, epistemology, and metaphysics? Did Aristotle's grossly wrong biology of reproduction really have any effect on his metaphysics? Is St. Thomas Aquinas's Christianization of that biology relevant to his theory of kingship or natural law? For modern philosophy, in which epistemology breaks free from religion and politics, the questions could be more persistent. Yes, perhaps it might be possible to see how a woman's supposedly inert womb relates to her inferior status, or how Eve's supposed fault in Eden might affect the Church's stand on women priests, but why would the personal foibles of a modern philosopher have anything to do with his reasoning about scientific method or the nature of reality? Can Kant's bitterness against women tell us anything about the categorical imperative? Can Hume's love affairs and friendships with women illuminate his moral sense approach to ethics? Can Rousseau's troubled youth say anything about the social contract?

For many philosophers committed to logical analysis, mixing biography with theory commits a fallacy. On this view the personal life of a man who holds a belief is irrelevant to whether that belief is well founded. A proposition's truth—the truth or falsity of Kant's claim that reason is the basis of morality or Hume's claim that justice is based on convenience—is logically independent of the experiential "genesis" of such ideas. How, why, or in what circumstances a philosopher comes up with an idea in no way determines the idea's value or truth. If Kant was a disappointed suitor, if Rousseau was a repressed hysteric, if Hume was a condescending ladies' man flattering the "fair sex," this has no bearing on philosophy. But for women reading philosophy, shaken by misogynous attitudes they found there, it was hard to get past the man to his supposedly gender-neutral philosophy. Why was Kant so insistent on an ethics that paid no debt to human nature or to passion, on an ethics that turned its back on sensuous life? What was the "nature of man" that had to be rejected by autonomous practical reason? Unable to occupy the position of either embittered suitor or urbane ladies' man, women were forced to question the experiential content of moral theories in a way that men were not.

At issue is not only the history of philosophy, but also the nature of philosophy. On one view the genesis of philosophy is in reason, in a philosopher's thought apart from his or her social status, sex, bodily habits, or constitution. The difference between Hume's and Kant's ethics is then one of definition and logic. The particular circumstances in which conflicting claims or arguments are made are irrelevant. Readers of philosophy learn to distinguish claims and evaluate arguments, skills that do not require knowledge of the private or personal lives of the men who made the claims. Feminist readings of philosophy that pay attention to gender relations challenge these standards of professional conduct, at the same time as they presuppose a different view of the role of philosophy. The shock of Hume's, Rousseau's, and Kant's treatment of women forces the realization that philosophy is not independent of experience. Hume's, Rousseau's, Kant's moral philosophy is a reflection on their lives as men, men in ambivalent contact with women, men with feelings as well as thoughts.

For some feminists this realization was enough to discredit philosophy altogether. If Hume's moral philosophy is the philosophy of a flirt, if Kant's philosophy is the philosophy of an embittered suitor worried about his virility, if Rousseau is troubled by Oedipal longings, what relevance can that philosophy have for women? Modern philosophy, some women charged, projects ideals of autonomy, rational freedom, and unfeeling logic that not only come out of masculine experience, but also represent a pathological "flight from the feminine." Given that flight, the contradiction between universal principles and women's disenfranchisement and dependent status follows as a matter of course. Susan Okin in the introduction to her 1979 *Women in Western Political Thought* expressed what was becoming a common view of Kant among feminists:

> Kant uses the most inclusive terms of all for the subjects of his ethical and political theory; he even says that he is not confining his discussion to humans, but that it is applicable to "all rational beings." Subsequently, however, he proceeds to justify a double standard of sexual morality, to the extent that a woman is to be condoned for killing her illegitimate child because of her "duty" to uphold, at all costs, her "sexual honor." He also reaches the conclusion that the only characteristic that permanently disqualifies any person from citizenship in the state, and therefore from the obligation to obey only those laws to which consent has been given, is that of being born female.
>
> (*Women in Western Political Thought*, p. 6)

Certainly Kant's reference to female honor was alarming. Just as a man's manly honor when he is insulted by another man may require that he challenge the offender to a duel, said Kant, so a woman's sexual honor, when she gives birth out of wedlock, may be to commit infanticide (*Kant's Political Writings*, pp. 158–9). The explanation, said Okin, of such a deformation in moral judgment is that rationality, citizenship, and even humanity are defined in masculine terms. Only a man would see a woman's honor in those terms; only a man would equate fighting a duel with committing infanticide. One virtue of misogynous philosophy, for feminists like Okin, is that it allows documentation of such distortions in thinking. The moralizing of philosophers like Rousseau, Hume, and Kant can be a fertile source for the detection of conflicting attitudes toward women, attitudes that continue to restrict women's intellectual and social advancement. It is not just that women were and are seen as inferior. They are adored and condemned. They are feared and belittled. They are the subjects of jokes that at the same time presuppose women's mythic power over men.

Misogynous philosophy can also be canvassed for possible sources for resistance. Hume's attention to the restriction of women's lives and his acknowledgement of reason for protest on their part was taken by some feminists as philosophical support for a degree of feminine rebellion at least in domestic settings. Hume's insistence that feeling and not rationality is the basis for morality gave credence to "feminine" styles of moral deliberation, as might also Kant's early suggestions of a woman's "enlarged" moral sensitivity. Alternatively, universal principle can be a basis for an insistence on justice for all. Although Kant never considered that women might vote or participate in his ideal kingdom of ends, his categorical imperative might be adapted as an argument for the equal treatment of women. Even Kant's comments on the indignity of being used sexually might be used by feminist philosophers thinking about sexual abuse and exploitation (Barbara Herman, "Could It Be Worth Thinking about Kant on Sex and Marriage" in Anthony and Witt (eds), *A Mind of One's Own*).

Beyond these uses of philosophy for the documentation of oppression or as a resource for feminist resistance is a further possibility. Attention to misogyny might have the virtue of leading to a deeper understanding of philosophy. On the simplest level, a discovery of neglected aspects of a philosopher's work, including parts rejected as non-philosophical, can put philosophy in a different light. A focus on Kant's comments on women, for example, reveals a moral thought that did not appear fully fashioned as a

result of logical analysis, but that developed out of personal and social experiences as a man, a professor, and a public figure. On this view, to look at the
"genesis" of ideas is not to commit a fallacy but to understand what philosophy is about. Why is autonomy and freedom so important to Kant? What
are the reasons, if not the arguments, behind an ethics that denies all influence to the body or to feeling? Kant's painful realization of the way we are
manipulated by passion, made to look fools, made to suffer indignities, his
sense that there is something degrading in being used, especially when that
use is sexual, places the categorical imperative in a different light. Commentators have often noted the intransigence of Kantian duty. Kant's misogyny
makes that intransigence understandable. Moral will must match in blinding
necessity what Kant experienced as the overwhelming and degrading
imperatives of sexual passion.

Past philosophers have often been used as targets on which students practice and sharpen critical skills. A universal principle that must never be
broken? But what if the Gestapo is at your door asking if you are harboring
Jews? Hume bases morality on moral sentiment? But what about a psycho-
path who enjoys killing? Generations of philosophy students have been
challenged to come up with similar counter-examples. Understanding the
genesis of moral theory suggests other kinds of exercises. What is one to do
about passion, which "always presupposes a maxim of the subject, namely,
to act according to a purpose prescribed for him by his inclination" (*Anthropology*, p. 73)? If in the throes of passion everything is sacrificed and one must
take possession of the object of passion, what alternative is there, if not a
categorical imperative that counters this necessity, a substitute necessity that
allows a person to exercise his or her will on a higher level with no resistance from material reality?

One of Kant's arguments for the separation of reason from physical life is
the failure of reason in practical life, a failure Kant himself experienced and
found unacceptable. He had reasoned. He was hesitant about marriage. He
made no impetuous moves. In the end, he might have been better off a
simple irrational peasant. The common man with little rational capacity, Kant
lamented, is happier than thinking, educated man. Reason can "reduce to
less than nothing . . . the advancement of happiness," it can kill off the
tender emotions, it can make a man miserable and misanthropic, even a
hater of reason. "By temperament cold and indifferent to the suffering of
others, perhaps because he is provided with special gifts of patience and for-
titude and expects or even requires that others have the same": a man like

this has no alternative but to find moral worth elsewhere in alienated reason (*Foundations of the Metaphysics of Morals*, pp. 11–15).

Given understanding of the genesis of moral theory, further questions can be asked. Were there other alternatives, alternatives that Kant himself considered before his views on women hardened into prejudice? Could there have been instead of the wholesale rejection of feeling, ways in which feeling is enlarged, expanded, and moderated so as to transcend narrow self-interest? Might a sense of the communicable "beauty" of moral character be a way to achieve generality in direct feeling response? A generative account of moral ideas not only elucidates the material content of a final moral position, it can also be a way to identify alternative lines of thought that a philosopher's final position obscures.

A philosopher's experiences in society and with women can be the basis for deeper interpretations of modernism itself. Alan Bloom in the introduction to his translation of *Emile* is no feminist; he applauds rather than condemns Rousseau's misogyny. But he also places Rousseau's and presumably other modern philosophers' troubled views on women at the center of a modernist dilemma. "No segment of *Emile*," said Bloom, "is more relevant than this admittedly 'sexist' discussion of the education of the perfect mate for modern man." Here, said Bloom, is an antifeminist argument that cannot be easily rejected because it is not based on biblical or ancient sources. Rousseau saw that modernism would destroy differences of sex, class, race, nationality, said Bloom. Everyone would become the "selfish Hobbesian individual, striving for self-preservation, comfort, and power after power" (*Emile*, p. 24). Bloom deplores with Rousseau the result: decay of the patriarchal family, which is the only place left where self-sacrifice or altruism can be taught or practiced. Each person becomes a "separate machine whose only function is to preserve itself, making use of everything around it to that end" (p. 25). For Rousseau, marriage and family play the impossible role of repairing the damage. Beneath whatever psychological pathologies or conflicts result from such a situation when women assert their rights, Bloom diagnosed a deep philosophical tension. Troubled relations between men and women are a "crucial point" at which the demands of the new modern individual with his tumultuous inner life and the demands of modern society engage. How can the self-interested entrepreneur be made into a dutiful citizen? How can the passionate appetite of men be satisfied in an orderly society?

The arguments of past philosophers can provide targets on which students practice their skills. The convictions of past philosophers can give credence to current theories. Philosophers' writings can be treated as texts to be deconstructed. Differences between Kantian deontology, Humean moral sense, or Rousseau's general will can be formulated, read back on history, and used to determine a set schedule of readings and interpretations. Feminist and non-feminist "anthropological" readings of Kant, Hume, and other philosophers complicate these formulas. Kant is not an opponent of Hume; he adopts Hume's views as his own. As his own social and academic life evolves along lines very different from Hume's, his ideas change and develop, are colored and transformed by his different temperament and experience. Such interpretations can seem a sacrilege. Icons are not men with clay feet and love affairs. To relate philosophy to ailing bodies, sexual impulse, or dinner parties can seem to trivialize and relativize, but for feminists, reading philosophy with new sensitivities and aspirations, it could seem that philosophy was coming back to life.

Further reading

A good introduction to the intellectual and social context of Kant's philosophical work is Manfred Kuehn's biography, *Kant*. Kuehn considers the incident with Maria Charlotta on pp. 167–9. The standard and most complete biography of Hume is by Ernest Mossner, *The Life of David Hume*. Mossner includes decorous but detailed descriptions of Hume's relations with women. Rousseau speaks for himself in his *Confessions*, which makes interesting reading in the light of Wollstonecraft's comments.

Hume's *Essays*, seldom read in philosophy classes, made his reputation and his fortune. Their publication and the time Hume spent revising and editing for subsequent editions reflect his conviction that philosophers should appeal to a wider audience. Interestingly, the essays that feminists have tended to cite as sympathetic to women, "Of Moral Prejudices," "Of Love and Marriage," were later withdrawn or deleted by Hume, deletions which Mossner insists (p. 141) were due not to the ideas, but to the playful style that Hume tried out and rejected as frivolous. The 1987 Liberty Classics edition, referred to above, is based on a posthumous edition, carefully re-edited by Hume for the final time before his death, but it also contains the withdrawn or deleted essays.

A full range of feminist philosophical response to Kant and Hume, including most of the viewpoints mentioned in this chapter, can be found in two volumes, *Feminist Interpretations of Immanuel Kant* edited by Robin May Schott and *Feminist Interpretations of David Hume* edited by Anne Jacobson. Additional articles on Hume and on Kant can be found in *Modern Engendering: Critical Feminist Readings in Modern Western Philosophy* edited by Bat-Ami Bar On.

2

DESCARTES

Man of reason

Where does philosophy come from? Does it come out of human experience, an extension of ordinary human abilities to respond and reflect? Is an *Enquiry* or a *Metaphysics* a personal statement: Here is how I, a man, lived or tried to live, in my time, in my place, in my social milieu, in my part of the world? Is philosophy then indistinguishable from expressive essay writing, autobiography, or story telling? If so it seems that philosophy can make little claim to truth. If Kant and Hume write out of their own experience in the eighteenth century, it may have little relevance in the present. If they write about their experience as men of a certain class, it may have little relevance for women or working people. Their world is not our world. We are unlikely to be enchanted by countesses in Parisian salons or devastated by sexual scandal in Königsberg.

It is precisely the disavowal of contingency and dependence that informs many philosophers' sense of their discipline's identity and importance. The human agreeableness that is the basis for Hume's ethics should stand on its own, regardless of the charm of Hume the man. Reason provides the logical foundation for Kant's duty ethics, not one man's soured romantic ideals. Otherwise it seems that ethics is reduced to autobiography of antiquarian or literary interest only. The modern period begins with a sense of the dangers of such relativism. In Europe, with religious certainty gone, with the authority of the universal Catholic Church and the divine right of kings compromised, with even the heavens in doubt given new cosmologies, it could seem that nothing is real but a man's private and personal sensations and ideas. But if this is all, what happens to knowledge? Adrift in a bewildering flux of sensation, bombarded by inconsistent claims from unreliable authorities, nothing is certain.

His dramatic portrayal of this primal modern predicament makes Descartes the textbook choice for the first truly modern philosopher. Descartes will give the first rationalist answer to the anarchic skepticism of transitional figures like Montaigne and Gassendi. Descartes will define the opening thesis in modernist debate, the thesis to which succeeding empiricist and vitalist philosophies are responses. Descartes marks out the terrain on which the themes of modern philosophy will be developed: the constitution of physical reality, the justification of knowledge, the reality of the external world, the basis for moral judgment.

If philosophers like Kant or Hume had much to say about women, Descartes said nothing. He had few dealings with the opposite sex. He preferred to stay at home rather than to dine out in aristocratic households or socialize in fashionable salons. As a young man gambling and drinking halls were his preference, and later university and academic circles closed to women. One glancing affair with a servant woman produced an illegitimate daughter whom he supported financially at a distance for a few years. For most of his productive life, he sought peace in the Dutch countryside. Other than a seven-year correspondence and friendship with the Palatine Princess Elisabeth and a brief and ill-fated foray into court life under the patronage of Queen Christina of Sweden, he was a man's man.

In the extensive body of Descartes's writing on science, metaphysics, passions, and morality, there is no discourse on the nature of women, on the proper education for women, or on the pains and pleasures of marriage. Never does he speak of women with contempt and rancor, never does he gallantly patronize the fair sex. His *Discourse on Method*, traditional opening reading assignment in Modern Philosophy courses, outlines intellectual procedures presumably available to anyone regardless of class, gender, race, or ethnic origin. Descartes never mentions the inferior intellectual capacities of "savages" or the sexual habits of natives. He takes no apparent interest in travel literature or colonial affairs. "Good sense," he insists, "is the most evenly distributed commodity in the world . . . the power of judging rightly and of distinguishing the true from the false (which, properly speaking is what people call good sense or reason) is naturally equal in all men" (*Discourse*, I, 1–2, in *Works*). The reason for error, he said, is not lack of native ability but improper use of one's rational faculties. Reason distinguishes men from animals; "it exists whole and entire in each one of us" (*Discourse*, I, 2, in *Works*). Over and over, Descartes asserted the commonality and universality of rational capacity. "There does not exist the soul so ignoble, so firmly attached to objects of sense, that it does not sometimes turn away from these to aspire after some other greater good" (*Principles of Philosophy*, in *Works*, p. 205). No mind is incapable of acquiring knowledge, he insisted, as long as it is trained in the rejection of ideas not clearly understood, in attentive concentration, and in methodical investigation.

The popular movement of Cartesianism that gathered momentum after Descartes's death and that flourished in Parisian high society can be taken as proof of its founder's lack of prejudice. These were circles singularly open to and even dominated by women. Cartesianism inspired women like Mary Astell to argue that, given the universality of reason, women should be educated, trained to read critically, encouraged to reason in their religious and domestic duties, and allowed to choose a single life. The Cartesian François Poulain de la Barre ridiculed the irrationality of the assumption that women are inferior and cannot profit from education. Cartesian feminists were not radical in their politics; for the most part they tended to monarchist and conservative views, but they forced heated debates on women's education to which Locke, Hume, and Rousseau were later contributors.

Nevertheless, much of what makes modern philosophy unwelcoming to women has been laid at Descartes's door: Descartes, feminist critics have argued, defined a dualist metaphysics that objectifies the natural world for man to master and control. Descartes theorized a solipsistic consciousness, removed from passion and imagination. Descartes projected a lifeless mechanized cosmos. Descartes drove a wedge between feeling and knowing, creating a masculinist illusion of absolute truth. Cartesian ideals of objectivity, rationality, mechanism, and control are hallmarks of philosophy's masculinist identity.

One of the first critical treatments of Cartesian reason was Genevieve Lloyd's *The Man of Reason*. As philosophy is currently taught, said Lloyd, it is assumed without question that reason has no gender. The modern mind claims independence from the physical body, male or female, white or nonwhite; the mind has no sex, race, or caste. If this is true, asked Lloyd, why is it that women have found philosophic reason so difficult to achieve? Why is it that women seem to resist logical, objective thought detached from passion and personal involvement? One can say that in the past women were not permitted the education and position that would have allowed them to become rational philosophers and scientists, but even now when these fields are open to women, women are still underrepresented and are not regularly named among philosophy's leading thinkers. Philosophy textbooks do not include readings by women, except perhaps a few recently added selections on feminist political theory. In core areas like metaphysics, epistemology, and logic, women are not represented.

To probe deeper the reasons for this exclusion, Lloyd proposed a "historical treatment" of reason, itself controversial by "rational" standards. If reason is the means to universal truth, there should be no need for history. In some eras, reason may be defeated by dogma or superstition, but reason is reason and its truths are ahistorical. Descartes in his *Discourse on Method* made clear his own distrust of history. History, he said, reflecting on what he saw as defects in his education, leads reason astray, burdening it with past error that must be expunged in methodical doubt. History is innocent enough if used for amusement or out of antiquarian curiosity, but useless where knowledge is concerned. Reason must leave the past aside to begin afresh. It must begin free of error, basing conclusions only on clear and distinct ideas confirmed in carefully constructed experiments. Climate, geography, social role, religious conviction, are irrelevant to reason. Anyone can reason, in any time and in any place. No bodily disability, no lack of physical strength, no sexual difference makes any difference where reason is concerned.

But, argued Lloyd, Descartes's reason, when understood historically can be seen as a factor in women's lack of power. The separation of sexless mind from sexed body that would seem to qualify women for intellectual activity in theory, as a matter of fact worked to their detriment. Logically there is no reason why women cannot be Cartesian philosophers and scientists. But the metaphysical division Descartes made between subjective bodily feeling and objective intellectual reason—the very distinction that might seem to protect women from discrimination—created exclusive spheres of activity that could eventually be identified with female and male roles. In theory there is nothing that prevents a woman from living the life of the mind; practically and historically it was all but impossible, given her domestic and social commitments. Scientific reason, as a restricted activity removed from practical knowledge and skills, became the exclusive domain of men.

Lloyd's conclusion was chastening. The maleness of philosophical reason is not only in overtly misogynist attitudes such as those expressed by modern philosophers like Kant and Rousseau. These might be ignored or corrected. It is not even that ideals of reason have been formulated by men out of men's experience. The seemingly sexless separatist ideal of modernist reason—separation from feeling, politics, religious enthusiasm, self-interest—inevitably lines up with separatist social ideals. Reason, whatever Descartes intended, becomes manly reason; retrograde empathy and irrational spiritualism become feminine feeling. The great benefit of feminist historical hindsight, according to Lloyd, is that it allows one to grasp this "conjunction of the text with surrounding social structures—a configuration which often is visible only in retrospect" (*Man of Reason*, p. 109).

Lloyd was aware of the dissonance between such a claim and the post-Cartesian analytic paradigm in English-speaking philosophy. Wasn't this to import politics into philosophy? Were not she and other feminist critics guilty of a distorted, self-serving slant on history? But, answered Lloyd, the analytic view of philosophical history—a series of logical moves from rationalism, to increased reliance on sensory experience, to the innovations of mathematical logic, logical positivism and naturalized epistemology—is itself the result of present professional commitments. Philosophical history, she concluded, is always subject to "tension between the need to confront past ideals with perspectives drawn from the present, and, on the other hand, an equally strong demand to present fairly what the authors took themselves to be doing" (*Man of Reason*, p. 110). The difference that distinguishes feminist histories is their lack of illusion. Feminist positioning in the present is self-conscious rather than unconscious and unacknowledged as it often is in the philosophical establishment.

More is at stake in this dispute than the role of women in philosophy. What is the correct relation between a student of philosophy and philosophy's history? Is it an illusion to think that a historian does more than create a past for herself and her constituency, a story that validates her or their present position and priorities? Or alternatively, should a historian's concern be objective scholarship, accurate portrayal of the thinking of past philosophers as historical artifact, embedded in its own cultural and intellectual context, factoring out present concerns as much as possible? What present theories can be used legitimately as neutral tools of analysis in the service of historical analysis? Which theories carry the contagion of present preoccupations and so taint the subject matter they are meant to illuminate? Logical analysis seemed to many analytic philosophers to provide the only clean tools. Look objectively at what a philosopher actually claims and argues. Leave doubtful connections with biography or social conditions aside. Examine terms for equivocation and vagueness. Note where proper definitions have been given. Check various propositions for consistency. Examine inferences for invalidity. Compare conclusions to other conclusions, present or past. In more or less pure form, such analyses make up a large part of current philosophical commentary. To bring in a concordance of philosophical categories with social roles, as Lloyd did, could seem an illegitimate move away from philosophy's history to social history.

Other feminist philosophers in the 1980s moved further from the analytic model in their commentaries on Descartes. In her 1987 *The Flight to Objectivity* Susan Bordo used theoretical tools even more controversial than Lloyd's social role theory. It is impossible, she argued, to "adequately identify, interpret or appreciate philosophical arguments, so long as they are viewed as timeless, culturally disembodied events" (*Flight to Objectivity*, p. 3). Descartes's skeptical arguments in his *Meditations* only make sense if understood in cultural context. As the *Meditations* is traditionally taught, Descartes doubts he has a body, suspects that an evil demon is tampering with his mind, imagines that all his experience is a dream, and concludes that the only thing he can be sure of is that he is a disembodied mind. This makes Descartes seem simply mad, or as many students comment, "on drugs." But when viewed in cultural context, said Bordo, "his arguments emerge as inventive, ingenious, and often beautifully concise expressions of and strategies for dealing with cultural crisis" (*Flight to Objectivity*, p. 3). What is in question, said Bordo, is not just the seventeenth-century disintegration of the Ptolemaic universe or the splintering of Christianity into warring sects. The *Meditations* express the psychological effect of radical changes in worldview, which create and continue to create a collective modern mental state of anxiety, dread, escapism, and schizoid vacillation. Using terms borrowed from psychoanalytic theory, object relations psychology, and cognitive psychology as "hermeneutic" tools, Bordo proceeded to psychoanalyze Cartesianism as the expression of symptoms of a culture in crisis. Cartesianism, argued Bordo, can be understood as "reaction-formation to epistemological insecurity and uncertainty" (*Flight to Objectivity*, p. 4).

Bordo used theories of child development, especially of the structural psychologist Jean Piaget, to provide a "narrative framework" for modernist history. She described a collective birth anxiety as culture passed from the middle ages and what she described as a feminine, intuitive, empathetic relation to nature to the objectified cognitive style of modern science. But, said Bordo, the passage as represented in Descartes's *Meditations* is not normal development from childish ways of thought to mature rationality. It is delusional on a par with other signs of pathology in the seventeenth century such as witch-hunts or the rise in extremist religious enthusiasm. Instead of healthy separation from "mother" nature and a mature acceptance of the fragility of bodily existence and the fallibility of knowledge claims, Descartes projects a delusional self, utterly separate from the body, capable of knowing certain truth, immortal master of a mechanized and therefore controllable nature. Lloyd was wrong to think that philosophy always tended to exclude the feminine, Bordo said. Premodern philosophies had feminine elements. Behind the imposition of Cartesian rationality that dominates current philosophy is another hermetic intuitive way of knowing more congenial to women.

Bordo's focusing of a variety of current theorizing about intellectual history and masculine psychology on a major philosopher, perhaps the major modern philosopher, was of course as unorthodox as Lloyd's social analysis. Bordo herself admitted some of the limitations. Her account, she said, was not meant to be a history of the past at all, and not meant to be the complete or only story of the origins of modernism. Rather it was a "selective" account of aspects of past events that survive in the present, aspects that continue to "make a claim on our attention" and endure as "artifacts of an upper-class, white, male, culture" (Flight to Objectivity, p. 5). Nor had she meant to give an account of the whole of Descartes's philosophy but only of one book, the Meditations. In fact, it was not really Descartes himself who was in question, she said, but her male colleagues still under the spell of Cartesian illusion. They were the ones she asked to look back to their intellectual past, to discover and overcome a pathology that continued to distort their thinking and make philosophy uncongenial to women.

Citing postmodern figures such as Foucault and French feminist theorist Julia Kristeva, Bordo expressed doubt whether any other more objective approach to history was possible. From a postmodern perspective, all we have is the present, the present text of Descartes's Discourse and Meditations, dutifully read and reread by philosophy students everywhere in the English-speaking world. We have no access to the vanished world of the past, no way of knowing how it felt to live in the shadow of the Jesuits or under the censorship of the Catholic Church. What we have is present theory, present texts, and present consciousness. In a bold reweaving of contemporary lines of feminist critical theory, psychological theory, and historical interpretation Bordo offered readers entry to the nightmare world of doubt that she believed underlies and is the pretext for contemporary rationalism.

One distinctive characteristic of feminist approaches like Bordo's was their interdisciplinary mingling of philosophical theory with theory from other fields. Philosophy in the postwar era took pride in its "professionalism," in having marked out terrain for itself in the face of the importance of technology and science in university curricula. Philosophy could not replace science, or reclaim the many areas taken over by science, but with specialized tools of analysis it claimed a role as an important aid to science. It could continue to expose obscurantist metaphysics that gets in the way of science. It could point out mistakes in logic that might occur in specialized areas such as biology, linguistics, or sociology. As the natural sciences challenged and won philosophical terrain, the defense of disciplinal boundaries was to many philosophers a necessary defense of philosophy itself. Descartes should be read accordingly, using properly philosophical tools of logical analysis. Is what is said true? Are the arguments valid? Is there a fallacy in Descartes's arguments for the existence of God? Can his "dreaming" argument be refuted? These are the questions that require philosophic skill, but it was just this sort of atemporal logical critique that Bordo disavowed in favor of psycho-cultural interpretation.

A second line of questioning concerned Bordo's use of psychology. The theories used by Bordo to further present understanding of Descartes could themselves be seen as artifacts of particular moments in history. Jean Piaget's developmental structuralism, Winnicott's object relations, Nancy Chodorow's update of object relations theory in light of feminist consciousness in the 1960s: these relatively recent approaches in psychology might be used to analyze present understanding of Descartes, as they might be used to analyze present understanding of anything. They might even be used in collective psychotherapy to cure a hysterical "flight from the feminine." But it was not clear what relevance such theories could have when projected back on to the seventeenth century. Bordo, it seemed, could herself be accused, not of presuming the universality of philosophy, but of presuming the universality of particular variants of psychological theory.

In defense, Bordo explained her "historical" use of psychological theory. Psychological theory, she said, allowed her to treat ideas not as timeless entities, but as changing in the course of human development. The individual development theorized in psychology could be read on to history to show ideas in process. With the framework provided by developmental psychology and object relations psychology, ideas could be seen to evolve, change, go into crisis, become complexes, be repressed. Ideas could be understood as the outcome of changing relations between self and world.

The question remained. Can contemporary theories of personality or masculinity be applied to men of all ages? The philosophers who were Bordo's contemporaries, raised in the contemporary nuclear family, nurtured

41

exclusively by mothers, forced out into lonely competition with men, might indeed be prone to various deformations of character. But Descartes, as a member of the minor gentry in the seventeenth century, had a very different kind of upbringing. His mother died shortly after he was born. Like many male children he was sent away to school at an early age. He was soon estranged from his father and all remaining relatives. His relational world was the world of the college and university, learned circles, and a few male friends. In this milieu, proof in geometry was not, it would seem, an escape from mother love, which he had never known, but a way to excel in academic circles and lay foundations for techniques and machines he was sure would revolutionize work and radically improve medical practice.

But, Bordo made clear, it was not Descartes, not this particular researcher and medical advisor with his interests in optics, algebra, and cosmology, who was her subject. It was her Descartes, the Descartes she and other women students had been required to study, admire, and refute. It was Descartes of the *Meditations*, standard opening text in philosophy courses. On this basis, Bordo could defend her psycho-cultural interpretation of Cartesian philosophy against Descartes's own account of what he was doing. The radical doubt of the *Meditations*, Descartes said, is strategic, provisional, entertained only so as to arrive eventually at a clear and distinct idea of God's necessary existence and the truth of explanations that have the clarity and distinctness of mathematics. There is no evidence that Descartes was doubtful of the truths of Catholicism, or that he suffered from a crisis of faith. His enemy in the *Meditations* is official misguided unthinking superstition, which in Descartes's mind has no intellectual standing.

In a move that would become popular with feminist philosophers, it was not so much the arguments but the literary flourishes in the *Meditations* that Bordo found revealing: the mad man who thinks he is made of glass, the paranoid sense of sensory deception, the insomniac who thinks the hand before him is not his. These colorful references allowed Bordo her cultural thesis. Even if Descartes, the man, did not himself experience such paranoid fancies, the images he used were generated in the collective consciousness of the seventeenth-century European mind. Bordo's aim, she said, was to provide access to that world, to make her colleagues feel the anxiety that forced the male philosophical mind into alienated rationality.

Another woman philosopher reading Descartes several decades earlier positioned herself differently. Simone Weil, writing a dissertation at the Ecole Normale in Paris did not, any more than Bordo, claim to give the one true and complete account of Descartes's philosophy. She too was acutely aware of a present vantage point, this time the great depression of the 1930s and the growing threat of Nazism. She was even willing to give considerable credit to analytic readings of Cartesian philosophy. Descartes, she said, does lay foundations for an abstract mathematical science divorced from working life and ordinary perception. Descartes is the textbook rationalist who bases knowledge on innate ideas and deduction rather than on experience and feeling. But, said Weil, a "careful" reading of the whole body of Descartes's writing reveals passages in "tension" with the standard interpretation. In fact, Descartes's main interests were not in abstract metaphysics or logic, but in medicine and other applications of science. She pointed to many examples used by Descartes from trades such as weaving or the making of eyeglasses. She cited his constant references to the movements of ordinary objects and his insistence that contact with physical reality is essential to understanding reality. Descartes's interest in mathematics, claimed Weil, was an interest not in "numbers" or math as the "language" of rationalist science, but rather in the fundamental mathematical basis of any methodical approach to physical reality.

Bordo focused on texts traditionally assigned in philosophy class, the *Meditations* or the *Discourse on Method*, written in an attempt to make the new science palatable to religious authorities. Weil looked to other less assigned works—the *Principles of Philosophy* and *Rules for the Direction of the Mind*, where a more practicalist account of reason emerges. Philosophy, Descartes made clear in the first lines of the *Principles*, is not properly an arcane technical discipline, but "what one needs to know for the conduct of his life and for the conservation of his health and the invention of all the arts" (*Principles*, in *Works*, p. 203). It is to accomplish this practical aim that knowledge must be based on principles that are clear and evident. It is for this that knowledge cannot be a piecemeal collection of supposed facts and truths, unrelated to each other, derived from a variety of authorities, and untested by experience. Unsystematic knowledge can give no real methodical understanding of phenomena like weight, gravity, atoms, heat, or natural substances. The natural world is a whole; its various parts interact one with another. These interactions are regulated by underlying physical principles that unite all of nature and are the basis for useful methodologies. What stands in the way of a practical science and philosophy, for Descartes, is not "feminized" tenets of medieval homeopathy, alchemy, or astrology, but professional philosophers of the academic establishment who abdicate responsibility as guardians of knowledge, leaving a vacuum in which ill-founded enthusiasms can take hold.

Descartes's main opponents, as he saw it, were the very academics that Bordo also opposed, logicians and dialecticians who, with syllogistic formulas and endless tricks of argument, obscure the truth. Logical disputation, said Descartes, might be all right for "school boys" (*Rules*, in *Works*, p. 4). It might keep university students occupied and out of trouble. It might provide some mental exercise. As a way to knowledge it is useless and even detrimental. Reason is better off without logicians who "prescribe formulae which are supposed to lend certainty to a necessary conclusion." When reason "commits itself to their trust" attention can be shaken and reality completely escape, especially when the premises on which arguments depend are unclear in meaning and uncertain in truth (*Rules*, in *Works*, p. 32). Logic can do no more than draw out what is already in premises. It is not a means for discovering the truth. Worse, it can guard and entrench error (*Rules*, in *Works*, p. 5).

The proper methodical approach involves first the grasp of first principles and second a moving from those principles to specific truths about nature, said Descartes. In both cases intuition plays a role, not as introspection of a preformed idea or object of thought, but as a mental act of attention and concentration. Against both received truths and groundless conjecture, Descartes proposed the grasp of truth by an "attentive and unclouded mind" on the model of arithmetic and geometry (*Rules*, in *Works*, p. 7). For Descartes, said Weil, mathematics is not the logically ordered language of textbook science, but a science of reality as practiced in master crafts such as optics, music, astronomy; it is the study of "orderly systems," such as are used by "craftsmen who weave webs and tapestry" or "women who embroider or use thread with infinite modification of texture" (*Rules*, in *Works*, p. 31).

Weil was not, any more than was Bordo, Foucault's naïve and old-fashioned historian insistent on making coherent, logically ordered, current sense of a man's philosophy, but nor was she a postmodern weaver of discursive patterns or a psychoanalyst of culture. Acknowledging that in some passages Descartes did seem to recommend a reasoning alienated from the body and the material world, she looked for conflicting currents of thought that lead in other directions. Would science become an abstract body of theory logically distinct from technical application? Or would a truly practicalist science evolve rooted in working life? Although for the most part the first alternative had won out, the second alternative remained a submerged and revolutionary possibility. Looking back not to an abandoned premodern past but rather to tensions within modernism itself, Weil drew out of Descartes a woman-friendly and worker-friendly vision of science with its own historical roots in Cartesian thought. In concrete practical interaction with physical reality in work and production, scientists could join with working communities of women and men to create new and progressive means of interacting with the physical world. The Cartesian revolution was no finished historical fact ready to be understood but a continuing process.

In most histories of philosophy, including many feminist histories, past philosophers are identified as villains or heroes. Some philosophers are applauded for getting it more or less right; others are blamed for getting it more or less wrong. Lloyd credited Descartes with gender neutrality but indicts him for a misguided dualism that provided the intellectual space for a schism between male and female roles. Bordo exposed a Descartes caught up in delusive reaction to cultural crisis. Weil, on the other hand, refused the adversarial position. For her, philosophy was a collective effort which she and others in the present were expected to continue. Not distancing herself as removed critic, she placed herself in the philosophical past, in tension with tendencies with which she was not in sympathy, looking for progressive tendencies which might move epistemology forward in the direction of a worker's science. For Bordo modernism reflects an alien masculine consciousness that has to give up Cartesian illusion and return to a repressed premodern past. Weil allied herself with modernity, but in the alliance she in the present took the leading hand. As the latest in a line of Cartesian philosophers, she took on the responsibility to retrace and redirect the path of philosophy. Purged was Descartes's famous dualism, that moment when in order to preserve an immortal soul and pave the way for Jesuit acceptance of science, Descartes claimed the mind's independence from the body. Weil's Cartesian method is embodied, its clear and distinct mathematics as much an aspect of physical reality as it is of the human mind.

Collaboration with a woman thinker had historical precedent in Descartes's case. Descartes's correspondence and friendship with the Palatine Princess Elisabeth was an important factor in his later work on ethics and emotion. Elisabeth, burdened with political, social, and familial responsibilities, was never able to devote herself to scholarship, but for several years, at the apex of his powers, Descartes accepted her as a supportive colleague and valuable critic. Her complaint that reason cannot be detached from the body and the emotions forced Descartes to confront the existential and ethical consequences of rationalist epistemology, and inspired a major work, *The Passions of the Soul*. From the standpoint of reason, maintained Descartes, one can observe tragic events as if at the theater. One can assess possibilities for action that bring about the best possible result and act without regret, regardless of the consequences. Elisabeth's questions remained. Can one really afford a purely cerebral rational approach in moral or political decision-making? Is not experience necessary in order to make political and moral judgments that have good results? Is it really possible to do away with divine Providence? Such an exclusive dependence on reason might be possible for Descartes, removed from public affairs in his country house, said Elisabeth, but not for a woman, or a man, involved in family and political affairs.

As Lloyd pointed out, pursuing such questions in the new scientific age would be difficult for women. Aristocratic privilege, which gave Elisabeth the opportunity for higher education, was fast disappearing in the new democratic republics of the eighteenth century. In coming centuries, Descartes's science would triumph over Aristotelianism and bring about radical changes in both university curricula and working life, and women would not, for the most part, play a leading role in that revolution. Could they have been or could they yet be among the innovators that run the experiments, debate questions of metaphysics, collect the specimens, construct the theories? The answer to these questions lies not so much in the quantifiable state of nature as conceived by Descartes, as it does in a "state of nature" that owes no debt to mathematical physics.

Further reading

On the role of Cartesian women see Carolyn Lougee's *Le Paradis des femmes* and Hilda Smith's *Reason's Disciples: Seventeenth Century English Feminists*. Margaret Atherton defends Cartesianism against feminist critique in "Cartesian Reason and Gendered Reason," an essay that appears in a collection generally supportive of rationality as a value for women, edited by Louise Anthony and Charlotte Witt, *A Mind of One's Own: Feminist Essays on Reason and Objectivity*. See also, for a diversity of views, *Women and Reason*, edited by Elizabeth Harvey and Kathleen Okruhlik.

Classic treatments of masculine metaphors in early modern science can be found in Carolyn Merchant's *The Death of Nature* and Evelyn Fox Keller's *Reflections on Gender and Science*.

Weil's thesis on Descartes is reprinted in *Formative Writings*. An account of her neo-Cartesian philosophy can be found in Nye, *Philosophia*. See the translations of Elisabeth's letters to Descartes along with commentary on their philosophical differences in Nye, *The Princess and the Philosopher*.

3

JOHN LOCKE AND THE STATE OF NATURE

When Descartes died in 1650, John Locke was eighteen. He had read Descartes. He approved the new science and vaguely accepted the notion of innate ideas. Like Descartes he saw no apparent contradiction between scientific reason and royal authority or established religion. By the time he wrote his major works a decade later in the 1660s—*Two Treatises of Government* and *An Essay concerning Human Understanding*—a change had occurred in his thinking. There were no more innate ideas. At birth the mind is a blank slate. The basis of knowledge is human experience.

So appears John Locke, first in the celebrated line of British empiricists who cleared away the last remnants of medieval essence and put science on a solid experimental basis. For Locke reason was innate but not as necessary truths accessible to introspection. Reason is a human faculty, limited in scope and exercised at will. As a result, belief is always unsteady and fallible. Those who cannot or will not accept its limits, those who persist in fanatically defending or imposing dogmatic theological or metaphysical principles, can and should be resisted along with the clerical or monarchical institutions that support them. In this way, restraints on free inquiry will be lifted and proper productive use made of practical knowledge.

The reason for Locke's change of heart was less philosophical argument than politics. In 1667 Locke, an Anglican don, was hired as secretary to the powerful and wealthy Anthony Ashley Cooper, future Earl of Shaftesbury. Shaftesbury—leader of the opposition to the Stuart monarchy, avid encloser and developer of a vast hereditary domain, founder of the Carolina colony, promoter of free trade, mercantile profit, and colonial expansion—had more than an academic interest in epistemology. As the earl's resident philosopher, Locke's job was to fashion arguments that would discredit the earl's mon-archist enemies and justify a government friendly to the interests of property owners and entrepreneurs. Locke would provide the theoretical basis for transfer of power away from the king and royal bureaucracy and into the hands of landowners and merchants whose wealth and well-being would bring general welfare to England and to all the lands subject to Britain's sovereignty.

The duties attached to the post of the earl's philosopher were not only theoretical, Locke was his employer's spokesperson and agent in material as well as intellectual matters. He acted as secretary for and wrote the constitution for the Lords Proprietors of Carolina, a colony in which Shaftesbury was the leading figure. He served on the Council of Trade and on the Board of Trade and Plantations, agencies charged with administering the colonial policies that would make Britain an imperial power. With Shaftesbury in prison or a fugitive, Locke organized a clandestine movement with safe houses, secret codes, and mail drops to keep alive the rebellion against absolute monarchy.

But Locke's most enduring contribution to the cause was theoretical. In *Essay concerning Human Understanding* he provided the epistemological underpinnings for libertarian politics, removing rationalist support for absolutist moral and religious objections to individual freedom. There is no thinking, argued Locke, before experience gives a man something to think about. With the removal of any God-inscribed necessity, the last defense of dogmatism falls and with it the cancerous proliferation of deductive certainty. In *Two Treatises of Government*, he spelled out the political and social consequences. All men are equal and free to pursue their own interests; there can be no authority except by consent of the governed; government should be limited in power; the accumulation of property is a right inherent in nature.

In Locke's empiricist epistemology, experience and man's innate faculty of reason support the same primary and manipulatable physical qualities of extension, figure, and motion as are measured in Cartesian mathematics. Mathematical principle holds material reality in place and gives a solid foothold for calculated invention and increased productivity. But nature as understood in the new sciences was not the "nature" that was the basis for Locke's social principles. The bedrock on which Locke's social philosophy rests is a different "nature," a "state of nature," a state that men are "naturally" in before they have been restrained in their activities by despotic power. In political and social writings Locke cited this "nature" without apology and without reserve. The mathematical nature of material reality might provide for weapons, machines, and productive technologies; another "nature" determines the sort of life men should lead and the relations they should have with each other.

In the *Treatises of Government*, Locke referred to "nature" and its derivatives over and over. Men are "naturally" in a "state of nature." The state of nature is governed not by civil law but by "natural" law. Men are equal by "nature," free by "nature," and have a "natural" right to acquire property and a "natural" right to punish anyone who breaks the "natural" law (*Treatises* II, Sections 4–8). By "the fundamental law of nature" men may wage total war on whoever attacks them or attempts to restrict their freedom (*Treatises* II, 16–21).

Here nature is not mathematical principle but a mysterious and irresistible force underlying social life. It is a human species-nature, individualistic, striving, self-interested, and impulsive. It is a natural biological instinct that drives man to his first social tie of marriage. This nature is not deceptive appearance to be investigated, catalogued, studied so as to discover the ultimate structures that allow for its alteration or manipulation. Nothing can disprove or dislodge a man's natural right to administer his property and acquire more. Social arrangements can honor or distort this "nature"; they can never change it. No social reform can win against nature, and if any is tried, war can be declared as Shaftesbury declared war on the Stuart kings.

Locke's "nature" dictates that a man must enter, at least temporarily, a monogamous marriage with a woman, and it also dictates rights and duties in family life. A man has a "natural paternal right" to govern his children until the children come of age (*Treatises* II, Section 55). Nature requires that marriage be at least semi-permanent so that child-care is guaranteed. Conflicts "naturally" occur in such an association, and given the nature of men and women, there is a "foundation in nature" for a wife's subordination to her husband when there is a disagreement (*Treatises* I, 47). When there is a difference in understanding and in will between husband and wife, the decision "naturally" falls to the man's share (*Treatises* II, 82). In this dictate, nature lays down a "rule" which men as well as "inferior creatures" have no alternative but to obey (*Treatises* II, 79).

Locke's addition of slavery as an aspect of nature can come as a shock. Here was the man ready in the same breath to proclaim the very impossibility of political servitude, the illegitimacy of even consensual agreements to give over one's natural independence to another person. But in the case of slavery, political reality imposed on nature a conflicting rule. Slave owning colonists attracted to Shaftesbury's Carolina were "naturally" unwilling to give up their labor force. The profits in cotton and sugar that drew colonists to such ventures in the new world depended on slave labor. The protection of property in slaves was written into the Constitutions of the new colonies of Virginia and Carolina. On this crucial point, Locke, like others of his time and station, reverted to Aristotle. A "natural" law of war allows a victor to kill his enemies. He can spare their lives and take them as slaves. If slaves don't like it, they can choose to die instead (*Treatise*, II, Sections 23–4).

It is hard to believe that Locke's experience in the administration of colonial affairs or his reading of travel literature could have supported the thesis that victims of the West African slave trade were "captives taken in a just war." At least implicitly, another law of "nature" intervened. Locke tended to take a relatively enlightened view toward some native peoples, for example native Americans. If those in other lands are backward, he sometimes implied, it is not due to any defect in human nature, but rather to a lack of science and technology. Considering some of the practices in European countries there was even some reason to think, said the liberal Locke, "that the Woods and Forests where the irrational untaught Inhabitants keep right by following nature, are fitter to give us rules than cities and Palaces" (*Treatises* I, Section 58). Africans, however, were not the subjects of such favorable comparisons. Locke's views on slavery reflect the judgment common in Europe at the time. Africans are different in nature. Other native people might be converted to Christianity, hired as laborers, even introduced to science and made into enlightened farmers; Africans were a race apart.

If Locke put up more of a struggle against the assumption that the inequality of women was natural, it was not because sexual inequality was any less obvious to him or his patrons. For men of Locke's class, women's subordination was as self-evident as the necessity for slave labor. But here Locke had a different problem. The natural authority of the male head of the British household was being used to support a powerful and influential argument for monarchical power. Certainly the monarchist opposition would have found little advantage in the analogy of slavery; few Englishmen were willing to think of themselves as Aristotle's "natural slaves," even if their master was the king. But if Englishmen could not think of themselves as slaves, they could think of themselves as dutiful sons, obeying a revered father ordained by God and nature to be their leader and guardian. With this powerful image—the nation as a family with a wise father at the head, with subjects born to him, born for him to rule and protect—monarchists like Robert Filmer hoped to crush Shaftesbury's rebellion.

To clear the way for Shaftesbury's defense of property rights gained by acquisition as well as inheritance and for mechanisms of government designed to protect wealth, the association between despotic paternal power and political power had to be broken. This analogy between father right and royal absolutism was Locke's main target in his *Treatises of Government*. There is no analogy, Locke argued, and even if there were, the analogy would not support absolute power. A father has a right over his minor children until they come of age, but that right is temporary and does not include any absolute power over them. Even more important, a father's right over his children is not exclusive but is shared with the mother just as power in government must be shared.

Locke paid close attention to the religious arguments used by Filmer and others. Passages from Genesis, said Filmer, gave Adam dominion over the earth, and royal power was passed down through the ages by inheritance. But the pronouns in Genesis are plural, Locke pointed out. "Gave he them," means that any dominion given to Adam was shared with other men or even with Eve. Did God really say in Genesis that in punishment for Eve's disobedience, she was to be ruled by Adam? Did God say that Adam should be the sole ruler of the earth who would pass down authority to hereditary kings through the generations? No, scoffed Locke. How could anyone think that God's chastisement of Adam and Eve in the Garden of Eden meant that Adam should rule?

> 'Twould, I think, have been a hard matter for any Body, but our A. [Filmer], to have found out a Grant of *Monarchical Government to Adam* in these words, which were neither spoke to, nor of him; neither will any one, I suppose, by these Words, think the weaker Sex, as by a law so subjected to the Curse contained in them, that 'tis their duty not to endeavor to avoid it.
>
> (*Treatises* I, Section 47)

So Locke was forced to negotiate the compromising fact of women's inequality. When God condemned women to painful childbirth, God was only "foretelling" what would be the fate of women, announcing how he was going to order it "providentially" that a woman would be subject to her husband. Yes, Locke admitted, "Generally the Laws of Mankind and customs of Nations have ordered it so," and there is a "Foundation in Nature for it" (*Treatises* I, 47), but not by divine fiat, not by natural necessity.

This was treacherous ground. If nature was allowed to dictate women's subordination it might also dictate other forms of subordination. Carefully Locke had to pick a way between existing social norms and liberal logic. There can be no precedent in whatever natural authority a man has over his wife for a man's authority over other men. All husbands would have husbandly authority, so conjugal power is not political power. Although a man does have the rightful authority in matters within his family "as Proprietor of the Goods and Land there" and the right to "have his Will take place before that of his wife in all things of their common Concernment" (*Treatises* I, Section 48), this cannot mean that in family matters a man has a "political power of Life and Death" over his wife (*Treatises* I, 48). And even if nature, or God, "foretold" that woman's fate is subjection, would not women have a duty to try to avoid that subjection, even as he and Shaftesbury had a right to rebel against the king? What if science found a way so that childbirth was not painful? Must a woman refuse to avail herself of it because God ordained she give birth in painful labor? What if a marriage contract is written with specific terms giving a woman property rights? Should not individuals be allowed to make whatever agreements they like? Why should the woman not have an equal share of power over her children, when it is she who nourished them "out of her own substance?" (*Treatises* I, 55). Here Locke was ready to abandon Aristotle. How could any reasonable person accept the archaic Aristotelian biology that sees the mother's womb as only a vessel for a tiny homicule with a rational soul that has been put intact into a yet unformed embryo via a man's sperm? (*Treatises* I, 55).

Why all the circumvention? Why not argue simply and consistently for the natural equality of women as well as of men? But Locke had already gone far enough to shock his political constituency: A mother has shared authority over her children? The husband has no right over what by contract is retained as his wife's separate property? The husband has no power over his wife's life? The wife has in some cases a "natural" right as well as a legal right by contract or law to separate from her husband? Child custody can be decided in the mother's favor? Marriage for only a term may be justifiable once children are independent? And if this nod in the direction of divorce or worse was not enough Locke went on to suggest that any kind of marital arrangement that achieves the aim of marriage to protect children might be justified, even temporary marriage.

Marriage for the modern Locke is not the young Kant's sacred union. Nor is it Hume's amicable companionship. It is a contract with mutual consideration based on biological convenience. A woman requires protection and income while she cares for a child; a man requires someone to bear and raise his children. At the same time the marriage contract cannot be an ordinary commercial contract, because "nature" is still allowed to dictate some of the terms. No contract, commercial or marital, can prenegotiate all the disagreements that might arise; although husband and wife have a common concern in the children, they will sometimes disagree. In a commercial contract disagreement is resolved by negotiation or, failing that, by judicial process. When marriage partners disagree, "It therefore being necessary that the last determination—i.e., the rule—should be placed somewhere, it 'naturally' falls to the man's share, as the able and the stronger" (*Treatises* II, Section 82).

In passages like these, "nature" is at embarrassing odds with political purpose, and the simplest ways of resolving the inconsistency Locke cannot take. If natural freedom and equality apply only to men and Locke admits the subjection of women as a natural fact, the dangerous analogy between paternal power and political right is allowed to stand. Alternatively, if Locke maintains women's full equality he jeopardizes the liberal cause. It was certainly not the policy of the Shaftesbury party to argue the radical thesis of women's rights.

Can the glitch in foundational liberal theory be repaired? Is it only removable "moral prejudice" that prevents modern democratic theorists like Locke, or Hobbes or Rousseau, from following the logic of their arguments and granting full citizen rights to women? Or does the fault in social theory around which Locke so painfully maneuvers run deeper than male bias and inconsistency in logic?

This was the question asked by Susan Okin in one of the first contemporary feminist treatments of the history of modern political theory. Feminist historical work, said Okin, is not "an arcane academic pursuit." It is an "important means of comprehending and laying bare assumptions behind deeply rooted modes of thought that continue to affect people's lives in major ways" (*Women in Western Political Thought*, p. 3). For Okin, the historical question—could not Locke have simply acknowledged the equality of women?—is also a present question—why is it that after most legal restrictions on women have been removed, women still have so little power in science and industry as well as in government and politics? Is there something in the fundamental terms in which modern philosophers think about the individual and society, terms inherited from the great philosopher revolutionaries of the seventeenth and eighteenth centuries, that blocks women's equality even in the late twentieth century?

Okin and other feminist theorists pointed out obvious failures in logic. Locke, she said, sacrificed consistency to expediency. He asserted women's independence when it helped his case. He resorted to nature to preserve her domestic status. But, Okin went on, there is more wrong here than inconsistency. Locke's citizen property owner, asserting his right to acquire property and his right to political participation, is not, and cannot be, the autonomous individual that nature says he is. He is the head of a supportive household of disenfranchised wife, female relatives, servants, and in some cases slaves. Domestic work, unmentioned in Locke's political theory, makes the new civil society possible. A wife's labor in child rearing, education, and household management allows a male head of a household to conduct the nation's business and increase his wealth. The restriction of a wife's activities to the home and the social stigma attached to a woman's sexuality ensure that a man's sons will be his and grow up to inherit his acquired property. In addition, servants and slaves accomplish the menial labor necessary for his physical survival. There is no way that women, let alone servants and slaves, can be released for participation in entrepreneurial or political activities. The distinction between the private household in which women and lower-caste men supply the material means of life, and the public sphere in which rational privileged-class men devote themselves to business and the making of laws, is essential to democratic politics. If women are equal, the material support for political and entrepreneurial activity erodes. Men have to do housework and share child-care. Alternate kinds of family units have to be acknowledged. Women have to control their fertility. Services have to be provided in the public sphere to ease the burden of domestic labor, which requires taking men's private property in taxes. The illusion of a common mind between husband and wife has to be abandoned, along with the idea that the interests of women and property-less workers can be properly served by upper-class male politicians.

By the 1970s when Okin wrote, most of the reforms in marriage alluded to by Locke had been implemented in Western countries. Property in marriage was shared in law and by prenuptial contract. Divorce was available. Husbands could be convicted of domestic violence. Women had the legal control of their separate property and more than an equal right to custody of children in case of separation. Many women worked outside the home, blurring the line between the private and public spheres. As these changes accelerated, the inconsistencies noted by Okin only deepened. If women work outside the home, children are left alone and homes are less pleasant from the commercial world of acquisition and competition. If exploited as unpaid domestic workers, they are doubly exploited force where, because of the necessity of at least some child-care and housework, they can be recruited for underpaid temporary or service work. Women have the right to divorce abusive husbands, but they are impoverished as a result. If they are members of a contemporary "gentry" able to afford nannies and housekeepers, exploitation is displaced on to other women, a reserve labor force of poor women, often racially identified, working as cleaners, babysitters, and daycare workers without benefits or social security. Nor could Okin propose a clear solution. New forms of family arrangements, shared domestic duties, complete integration of the work force, reproductive rights, increased government services were visionary. Could these changes be accomplished within the structure of the capitalist economies tailored to Locke's competitive and individualist human nature? Okin doubted that they could.

Another feminist philosopher, Carol Pateman, working at the same time, focused on the idea of social contract so prominent in modernist social theories like Locke's. A man in Locke's "state of nature" is a solitary self-interested individual without social position or social obligations. In the new democratic theories, any obligation such a man takes on must be consensual, by agreement or contract. This premise generates the terms of legitimate political arrangement and mechanisms of popular control designed by Locke and other supporters of representative government. But before any such "social contract" is made, Pateman argued in *The Sexual Contract*, there has to have been another contract, a sexual contract that supports the marital arrangements and the sexual division of labor that Locke placed in the "state of nature" prior to any political social contract.

The basis of the marriage contract, for Locke, is convenience. If a man is to reproduce himself, he must procure not only sexual services but also care of resulting children. A long-term contract must be made for the domestic services of a wife. Can Locke's marriage contract be freely consensual on the part of both man and woman, negotiated by two individuals, free and on an equal footing? No, said Pateman, it cannot. The illusion that marriage is or could be a freely made contract covers over the underlying sexual consensus that fixes the roles of men and women prior to any civil union. A marriage must be heterosexual. A marriage cannot be a term marriage, made in contemplation of divorce. A marriage must include sexual fidelity on the part of a woman.

But why not? Cannot any arrangement be made between any individuals in these circumstances, between an individual rational man and woman, or between a couple of the same sex as long as children are provided for? Pateman's answer was no. The liberal feminist agenda of extending the status of autonomous free individual to women so as to make democratic theory consistent is a misguided goal, misguided because it ignores the fact of difference. Locke's modern individuals, the individuals who are to be the property owners and the citizens in the new modern states, have to be men. They have to be men because they are all the same; it is their very separation from the different world of women and the family that makes them individuals and the same. Here Pateman tapped what would become an important theme in feminist theory, the appreciation of difference. Women are bodily different. Women become pregnant. Women have the capacity to lactate. Women are not the same as men.

Neither Okin nor Pateman offered a clear solution. The problem for feminists was both theoretical and practical. Is the proper philosophical basis for feminist politics libertarian individualism expanded to include women as citizen property owners? Or should feminists turn to socialist or communist theories that presuppose a different communal "nature"? What should be the aim of a feminist politics? Equal rights? Or social welfare and a planned economy in which the state provides essential services and private family life as we know it disappears? As the communist bloc of states withered away in the 1980s the socialist solution seemed less and less tenable. Utopian Marxism had preached the dissolution of the family as an economic unit. In the new socialist states, men and women were to work on an equal footing; children were to be raised in state-financed child-care facilities; meals and housework were to be provided on a communal basis. Sexual relations would be free, committed or uncommitted in any ways that individuals desired. In fact, regardless of these visionary ideals, Pateman's sexual contract had held. In the new Soviet states, women worked a full day and went home to a full round of domestic work not shared by their husbands. Homes, allotted by the government, were no longer refuges, private spaces of relaxation and refreshment, but a few impoverished rooms in which women worked as they did before, only under even more difficult circumstances. In the workplace women were still clustered in lower-status jobs.

Socialist economics is not enough, said radical critics like Juliet Mitchell (*Women's Estate*). Locke's "natural" family has to change. A distinction must be made between child breeding, in which women "by nature" play the greater role, and child rearing, which is not naturally the job of women and can be shared by men. Psychologists projected the different psychological nature that might result in families where parenting is shared. If boys were brought up by fathers as well as mothers they would avoid the identity crisis that results when care giving is only from women. Girls would change as well with the increased confidence that comes from identification with ambitious fathers. An even more radical tampering with Locke's nature came from Shulamith Firestone in *The Dialectic of Sex*. Nature in the form of biology must be overcome, Firestone argued. Women and men can never be equal, as long as women spend nine months in pregnancy and several months recovering from birth. Shared parenting is not enough. Only biotechnology, Firestone projected, could solve the problem by allowing controlled gestation outside the womb. Once women were released from pregnancy, child-care could be accomplished by the state or in licensed households made up of freely contracting persons of any sex or age. At this vanishing point, little of Locke's nature remained; in its place was science fiction.

From what experiences had it come, this obdurate sense of what is real and natural and inevitable between men and women, no matter what individuals might freely will for themselves? Locke, like most of the educated persons of his time, was acutely aware of human diversity. The extensive collection of travel books in his library shows that he was interested and versed in exploration and discovery in foreign lands where European entrepreneurs and colonists found men and women living in a bewildering variety of circumstances. It is hard to see how any universal primal state could be abstracted from these experiences. Children, it was clear from reports of other societies, could be cared for in endless ways. The expression of sexuality took many forms and meanings. A variety of kinship structures were possible (matrilineal, polygamous, polyandric) and a variety of living conditions (patriarchal, patrilocal, matriarchal). In some societies, siblings lived together with husbands or wives, households were segregated by sex, premarital or extramarital sex was condoned. Rather than universalize about a "state of nature," Locke might have emphasized the historical variability of social arrangements, an approach more consistent with his own empiricist epistemology.

Locke himself described the danger in extracting a general idea from always limited experience. General ideas are abstracted from sensory experience, he said. From simple observations we move to similarities and then to general ideas. A child knows first her mother and nurse. As a consequence, her idea of "man" at that point may be purely feminine; men may seem to her to be foreign animals. Later she sees similarities between mother and father, and then between other relatives and acquaintances, and begins to broaden her idea of man. Basing reasoning on limited experience, warned Locke, can lead to error. Locke's example: if a little boy sees only white men, he may be able to demonstrate that a negro is not a man. Whiteness may seem to him to be a necessary characteristic of man, a conclusion that is clearly wrong. No necessary deduction from abstract ideas is possible because there is no necessary correspondence between such ideas and reality, only a similarity noted between a limited number of experiences, a similarity which later may prove misleading (*Essay concerning Human Understanding* Book IV, Chapter vii, Section16).

Challenged for concrete examples of the experiential basis of a 'state of nature," Locke offered two possibilities. First, he said, a state of nature exists between warring princes. This certainly had been, and would continue to be, an inescapable fact of European experience in the modern period. Peace in seventeenth- and eighteenth-century Europe was rare and short-lived. Successive wars ravaged the countryside and decimated the population. Once a state of war broke out, no law restrained the violence, only brute military power. Over and over, the social fabric of tradition and custom as well as economic infrastructures were torn apart in territorial wars driven by the ambitions of princes and fueled by sectarian zeal.

The second kind of example given by Locke is related to that rivalry, but on a different battleground, not Europe but the rich and profitable lands European powers were now vying to control. On a desert island off the coast of South America, a European is shipwrecked. Another man, also shipwrecked, shows up. On the island there is no sovereign state, no law. The two are in a state of nature; they must contract with each other for goods and services as best they can (*Treatises* II, Section 14). Or another example, a Swiss trapper meets an "Indian" in the woods of America. Again the Swiss must contract for furs or foodstuffs with the native without commercial regulation (*Treatises* II, 14). The experience from which Locke's state of nature was derived is European experience, experiences of devastating interdynastic war and the experiences of European travelers, explorers, colonists, slave traders, prospectors in non-European lands. "Nature" is not an abstract construct, nor is it an innate idea or deductive conclusion; it is a general idea based on certain experiences: on rivalry between European princes, stand-offs between European men on contested ground in the Caribbean, uneasy trades between local inhabitants and European colonists and adventurers in the Americas. In these "states of nature," contracts between individuals have to be made where there is no government recognized by Europeans. "Inconveniences" result when contracts cannot be enforced. Eventually some sort of social contract has to be made, a truce, an armistice, a colonial government or constitution, such as Locke had helped to institute in the Carolinas.

No matter how much generality is claimed for it, the "state of nature" is a European idea based on European experience. The native Carib or "Indian" experienced no state of nature; he was subject to community or tribal regulation. Locke's state of nature does not reflect his or her experience, only the experience of a particular group of men with whom Locke was associated, men engaged in the enterprise of profit making in colonial lands and empire building. "Nature" in this sense necessitates forms of family life. A soldier on campaign, an adventurer abroad, a businessman tending to his investments in European capitals is on his own with the freedom to make his fortune as best he can. But if he is to pass on the wealth he hopes to make, he needs a family ready to receive him, a family that is not expected to undergo the dangers and discomforts of exploration or war, or even in some cases the rigors of commercial life in the city. The size of a man's supportive establishment depends upon his own efforts and talents, talents that Locke freely admitted vary greatly from man to man. Certainly as the "abler and stronger" proprietor and acquirer of family property a man will expect to have the last say at home. Away from home, free and responsible for his own welfare, he may be forced to make some sort of social contract or colonial constitution with equally enterprising countrymen or with other Europeans in order to ensure that the property he acquires has the protection of law. He may have to see to it that kings no longer issue restrictive royal licenses or tax exports and imports. Spanish monarchs must no longer claim large territories by right of discovery. Indians must no longer occupy undeveloped land. Property holders must decide among themselves laws that will protect their property.

Later, in the nineteenth century, based on different experiences, rival accounts of "nature" were proposed. Using anthropologist Lewis Henry Morgan's 1877 account of native American communities in *Ancient Societies*, Marx and Engels challenged many of Locke's assumptions. Human nature, they concluded, is not individualistic and competitive; it is naturally social and cooperative before capitalism distorts it. The European bourgeoisie imposed on "nature" their own acquisitive greed. But even in Engels's socialist family, some of Locke's nature remained. Not nature, but men's institution of private property brought the "world historical defeat of the female sex," wrote Engels (*The Origin of the Family*, p. 120), but even in socialist society there is a natural division of labor in the family. Consistent with this natural separation of male and female roles, men would play the major role in the labor movement that was to lead to socialism.

But without a state of nature, or natural man, or any primal beginning point for social theory, on what can social philosophy be based? What can philosophy offer if it is not foundational theory from which a diagnosis of social ills can be made and a recipe for beneficial change? At stake in disputes about Locke's state of nature are not only gender equality but the nature and purpose of philosophy. Is philosophy with its grand conclusions useless now that empirically based but always provisional sciences of diverse human origins and social arrangements are available. Can one substitute for the philosopher's "state of nature" anthropological studies of the communal councils of Amazon Indians or the sexual habits of Polynesians. Is the best philosophy can offer a philosophy of anthropology or of biology that monitors for mistakes in logic or for theory that is underdetermined by evidence.

Feminist philosophers, wary of scientific authority that supports false theories of women's inferior nature, stand both to gain and lose from such restraint. On the one hand, logical scrutiny might show the lack of evidence supporting the universality of conservative views of male and female roles. Analysis might uncover inconsistencies in the ways societies are described. On the other, deference to existing methods of analysis and experimentation in science could further reinforce prejudices inherent in research. Philosophers like Okin and Pateman were more ambitious. Their target was not poorly done social research but conceptual tangles that govern current thinking about sex and that may distort even the most rigorously empirical studies. Okin, for example, hoped to shed light on the seemingly illogical alliance between current supporters of libertarian economics and defenders of conservative family values. Her analysis of Lockean themes shows how the two are in fact complementary; maintaining the patriarchal family is required if men are to exercise their economic freedoms. In reconsidering individualism, she made visible the cadre of domestic workers taken for granted by Locke and also by many present defenders of the accumulation of wealth. She called attention to migrant farm workers, domestic workers, sweatshop girls in peripheral economies who make up the massive exploited labor force of expendable individuals, cut loose from the security of traditional communities, whose underpaid labor contributes to Western capital wealth.

Here the role of historian of philosophy is neither modest handmaiden to social science nor presumptuous dictator of the foundations of justice in society. The study of philosophy elucidates contradictions in contemporary thought, contradictions with historical roots. If marriage is no longer a sacred icon in Locke's secular modern state, its terms are still dictated by natural law for many women and men. At the same time many marriages fail. Women have a right to divorce, but are impoverished by it. Children go hungry, resort to crime, never learn to read. The contemporary response is to blame individuals: women who refuse to work, men who desert their families, children who will not learn. If feminist philosophers like Okin and Pateman are right, the fault lies deeper in thinking about gender with roots in seventeenth- and eighteenth-century philosophy.

Pateman's analysis of the history of social contract theory brings into focus conflicting elements in contemporary marriage. The trappings of seventeenth-century arranged marriage are retained in many marriage rituals. The father of the bride "gives her away." The bride agrees to "honor and obey" her husband. The bride wears white, a symbol of protected virginity delivered intact by a father to her husband. These rituals are consistent with relations between wife and husband in Lockean marriage. The husband is the breadwinner, the acquirer of property. As the abler and stronger, he will have the last word in disputes. Although the wife may work to supplement household income, she will bear the responsibility for home and children. Any suggestion that a voluntary contract be drawn up on analogy with commercial contracts, with specific agreements as to place of residence, responsibility for domestic work, timing of children seems, given the assumed terms of Pateman's sexual contract, adversarial and antithetical to marital union.

Shulamith Firestone's radical proposals for abandonment of traditional "natural" marriage seemed hopelessly fictional in the 1970s when it was difficult to conceive the artificial means of reproduction that she projected were necessary to liberate women from pregnancy and initiate new forms of family life. Now in the first decade of the twenty-first century, biology has kept pace with science fiction. Cloning and in vitro fertilization make possible new artificial forms of reproduction. Lesbians and gays force consideration of the possibility of "unnatural" civil unions with or without children. Firestone's analysis of the restraint biology places on women, and the possibility of liberation from that restraint in biotechnology, further illuminates current political divisions, especially the intransigence of conservative resistance to abortion rights, and, more recently, to various forms of technologically assisted reproduction under the banner of right to life.

Crucial to these insights into contemporary debates between feminists and their opponents is a sense of the intellectual and material past of our present condition. The unstable twenty-first-century household in which women still struggle for equity has a philosophical past in Locke's state of nature. Present-day entrepreneurs still require the support of women and servants at home. The developing world is still Locke's "Woods and Forests," a zone known mostly second hand and through biased accounts. If poorer nations emulate Locke's natural enterprising man, they are promised Western prosperity. If Europeans are allowed to trade and barter and take over "wilderness" land for the rational extraction of sellable commodities, the woods and forests will prosper. Locke's Swiss trader exchanging beads for valuable furs in the woods of North America, his two Europeans fighting over control of a piece of tropical real estate, have become proxy wars with native troops, multinational franchises, and transplanted sweatshop production. If reading Locke from a feminist perspective does not offer a universal scheme for social reform, it brings a shock of understanding. Locke's state of nature, setting the terms for marriage relations and property rights, is not a determining and limiting "essence," but an abstract idea derived from experience that may turn out to be as limited and ultimately inadequate as a little English boy's insistence that all men are white.

Further reading

Peter Laslett's introduction to the *Two Treatises* gives an excellent introduction to the historical background of Locke's social theory. Especially interesting are Laslett's comments on and references to the Constitution of Carolina and Locke's Instructions to Governor Nicholson of Virginia (*Treatises*, pp. 302–3, note 24). Also of interest on Locke's involvement in British and colonial politics are Neal Wood's *John Locke and Agrarian Capitalism* and Barbara Arneil's *John Locke and America*.

For more feminist commentary on the family in modern social theory see Jean Bethke Elshtain's *The Family in Political Thought* and *Public Man, Private Woman*, and Linda Nicholson's *Gender and History: The Limits of Social Theory in the Age of the Family*. Lawrence Stone's *The Family, Sex, and Marriage in England 1500–1800* is a good source for general social and economic background.

4

REWORKING THE CANON

Anne Conway

The year was 1679. Shaftesbury, released from the Tower of London, called Locke back from exile in France to resume their struggle against absolute monarchy. That same year philosophers with very different interests met at the Imperial Abbey of Herford in the Rhineland. The abbess, Elisabeth Princess Palatine, Descartes's old friend and collaborator, lay dying. Among those attending at her deathbed were the adventurer-philosopher Francis Mercury van Helmont and the philosopher-diplomat Gottfried Leibniz. In addition to comforting and advising Elisabeth in her last days, Van Helmont was on a mission. He carried with him a manuscript written by his recently deceased friend, Anne Conway. Hoping to interest influential persons in Conway's ideas, looking for help in getting her book published, Van Helmont was especially anxious to show the manuscript to Leibniz. Van Helmont had worked closely with Conway in the last years of her life on a number of projects. For a period of time they shared an interest in Quakerism. They assisted their friend Christian Knorr Rosenroth in his translation and compilation of kabbalistic writings, published as *Kabbalah Denudata* or *The Kabbalah Unveiled*. They discussed at length the great issue of the day, the conflict between mechanistic science and religious metaphysics.

At Elisabeth's deathbed came together a confluence of diverse lines of thought. Elisabeth's doubts about metaphysical dualism and rationalist ethics were expressed in her philosophical letters to Descartes. Leibniz was deeply involved, as he would be throughout his life, in attempts to temper and modify Cartesianism so as to guard against atheism. Quakerism with its radical revisions of orthodox religion and its militantly egalitarian social philosophy left its mark on many present. Elisabeth had been friendly with several leading Quakers and had interceded on their behalf on several occasions. Van Helmont was a convert to Quakerism for a period of time.

Quakers provided comfort to Conway in her last illness. As always, Van Helmont's wide-ranging researches in spiritualism and the occult stimulated discussion and controversy. To add to the mix, Conway's unpublished manuscript was available for scrutiny.

When Conway's *The Principles of Most Ancient and Modern Philosophy* was finally published eleven years later, it made little impact. Leibniz retained an annotated copy and mentioned the work several times in passing as expressing views in some ways similar to his own. Henry More and Van Helmont promoted the book, but more as memorial to a great lady than as groundbreaking theory. Leibniz became a canonical figure in English-speaking philosophy, one of the major philosophers of the modern period. More won a place in philosophical history, if only for a temporary reversion to neo-Platonism. Even Princess Elisabeth achieved some small fame; several of her letters to Descartes would be quoted in biographies of the philosopher. In surveys of modern philosophy, Anne Conway was forgotten.

So goes the curious process of canon formation. Among the tumult of discordant voices and competing intellectual fashions of any historical period, ideas of lasting significance are extracted and highlighted. The selection process is complex. No committee or court sits once and for all to determine what will count as important philosophy. Many small decisions accumulate over time. Individual philosophers decide what they will include in syllabuses, what they will write about in journals and books, whom they will discuss in textbooks. Groups of philosophers in university departments and on editorial boards meet to determine what philosopher will be hired, whose books will be published, which papers will be accepted for reading at conferences. Eventually what is important begins to seem obvious. It becomes unthinkable to omit Descartes, Locke, or Hume from a reading list in modern philosophy. They define what philosophy is and what it is not. Standard excerpts from their writings reprinted in textbooks provide models by which to distinguish philosophy from polemic, religious writing, and literary essays.

Fame in one's own lifetime is not decisive. One of the advantages of history is hindsight, possible only when the dust of active disputation clears and lines of thought can be distinguished that have affinity with succeeding views or current views. Van Helmont for all his notoriety and his influence on his contemporaries, including canonical figures like Leibniz, is not on current reading lists in seventeenth-century philosophy. The neo-Platonism of Conway's early teacher Henry More with its magical numerology and cosmological allegories has few adherents and is not taken seriously. In a secular era Quakerism, a source of social and intellectual rebellion in the seventeenth century, is dismissed as a religious orientation not a philosophy. In a scientific age, Van Helmont's interest in sympathetic magic is pseudo-science not philosophy. So goes the rhetoric of canon formation.

But canons do not necessarily remain intact. As in sacred scriptural traditions, philosophy is periodically subject to reforming hermeneutics. The enduring themes of philosophy are interpreted in the present. As current practice and interests change, so do the historical sources of ideas. Ideas, no matter how revolutionary, require a past to give them content and substance. As Henry More said of his own historical work, he needed to find "god-fathers" for his ideas to give them depth and authenticity. In the process of canon formation and change, works that once seemed important can be eliminated as confused or antiquated. New works can be discovered more congenial to contemporary views. Old works can be reinterpreted in new ways. Parts of a recognized philosopher's work can be restored or factored out.

Leibniz is a case in point. At the height of the popularity of logical atomism and positivism in the 1930s, Bertrand Russell ruled out much of Leibniz's metaphysics as philosophically worthless. Putting aside Leibniz's interest in "unscientific" and "illogical" ideas like those of Van Helmont and More, Russell singled out one aspect of his early work as historically important. Leibniz did not, said Russell, make the mistake of condemning formal logic as useless. Instead he projected the very logical calculus that contemporary philosophers like Carnap, Whitehead, and Russell were developing. With logic as the centerpiece, a salvageable version of Leibnizian metaphysics was retained, founded in logic instead of religious or cosmological speculation.

So Leibniz took a new position in the narrative history of modern metaphysics. Descartes opens the field with his *Meditations* and *Discourse on Method*. In response to metaphysical dualism comes Hobbes's materialism and Berkeley's idealism. The metaphysical skepticism of Locke and Hume eliminates the last remnants of religious dogma. As the eighteenth century closes, an inkling of logical atomism with Leibniz is challenged but not defeated by a last gasp of substantive metaphysics in Kant's noumena and phenomena, a distinction that re-emerges purged of metaphysical content in the positivist's distinction between analytic and synthetic.

Russell's analytic history involved a considerable winnowing down of historical material. In the seventeenth and eighteenth centuries controversy was rampant. Burgeoning science in a bewildering variety of forms was on everyone's mind, along with the adjustments in thinking that scientific views of reality seemed to entail. Scientific questions and religious questions were hopelessly mixed. What kind of God was consistent with an infinite universe? How was a person to make decisions if she was only a bit of Descartes's extended matter? What was the effect of science on politics? Scientists in the early modern period were not a caste apart, immune from philosophical criticism, but active members of a wider learned community. Philosophers like Descartes, Leibniz, and Van Helmont were scientists, but took an active interest in politics and religion. As they did at Herford, women played active roles as patronesses, supporters, publicists, and also were active participants in many of these disputes.

In Russell's and other analytic histories there were no women's voices. In metaphysics this could seem less important than in politics. What is the nature of being? What are the ultimate constituents of reality? These are questions that seem dependent only on sexless reason for answers. Yes, perhaps Locke, an unmarried man, was unlikely to see marriage obligations in the same light as a woman even a woman of his own class. Yes, Rousseau, who insisted that his lover put their children into a foundling home, might not be the best person to describe the ideal moral education for women. But would a woman have anything to say about the ultimate constituents of reality that could not be said as well by a man? It seemed to many philosophers that, although women might have distinctive and valuable insights in social or political matters, in metaphysics Descartes, Locke, Leibniz, and Kant could speak for women as well as for men.

One way to challenge this assumption is critical and essentialist. Starting with an idea of what is "feminine" or a woman's "nature," one can claim that women experience the world differently from men, either because their social or biological roles differ or because they see things differently or think differently from men. Men's metaphysics then can be charged with a false universality that denies diversity. Much feminist commentary on Descartes has been in this vein. Descartes separates mind from body; women will not or cannot do this. Descartes relies on pure reason; women's intelligence is interactive and emotional. Similar feminist complaints are made about Locke. Locke begins with the idea that to be human is to be a self-interested individual; women with a less barricaded ego identity experience the social world in communitarian terms. In both cases, the experience and view of men of a particular class of society with particular interests cannot be taken as representative of the different point of view of a woman.

By the 1970s and 1980s feminist critical commentary of this sort had already begun to change a philosophical canon that includes interpretation as well as primary sources. Especially in the area of political philosophy, texts and readers were expanded to include at least token examples of feminist critique, such as Okin's treatment of Locke or Pateman's supposition of a "sexual contract." Canonical figures remained in place, but different aspects and sections of their writing were highlighted, challenging and deepening standard interpretations.

Another approach was more ambitious. Might it be possible to find actual women philosophers working in the modern period who might be included as major contributors to the history of philosophy? This project, undertaken by a number of feminist historians in the 1980s and 1990s, proved not to be an easy task. First, it was hard to find candidates for inclusion. The great majority of women in the seventeenth and eighteenth centuries did not have the educational or social advantages that would have allowed them to enter into philosophical debate on an equal basis or produce written treatises. Women did not attend universities, did not join Royal Societies, were not given academic posts. As a royal who might one day inherit a throne, Descartes's correspondent Elisabeth was an exception. She received a rigorous education along with her brothers in Latin, Greek, math, and science, an education very different from the training in docility and decorative arts recommended later by educational authorities like Rousseau. Van Helmont's protégé Anne Conway, as was more usual even among the aristocracy, received little formal schooling and was mostly self-taught, while her brother, an indifferent scholar, was sent to Cambridge. Only by unusual persistence and initiative did Conway manage to convince her brother's tutor, Henry More, to help her in reading Descartes.

When women in the seventeenth and eighteenth centuries did manage to gain access to philosophical ideas and produce written work, often their work remained unpublished or was destroyed or discarded. Of extensive correspondence between Conway and More, very few of Conway's letters survive, although many of More's are available. It was only by accident that the letters of Princess Elisabeth to Descartes were discovered in the drawer of an old secretaire. As with Elisabeth, social obligations and stress-related illness prevented Conway from organizing and editing material in her notebooks, as Van Helmont noted regretfully in his introduction to her *Principles*.

Even when a woman philosopher of note is identified, she can seldom be simply added on. A canon is not a list of disconnected names. Relations between thinkers, worked and reworked by generations of commentators, bond philosophical materials together in historical sequences with direction and meaning. A thinker critiques or responds to specified predecessors. He or she is a link in an ideological sequence, more or less linear, more or less progressive. Because a canon represents a line of thought with links to the present, just as with scriptural canons additions can cause reverberations up and down the line, both in accounts of ideas that predate the addition and in accounts of ideas that come after it. Adding to a canon often means revisions of past history and present history, as other additions and deletions, and other interpretations and judgments, become necessary to reshape a coherent succession of ideas.

In Conway's case, association with known figures such as More and Leibniz helps. She can be placed, probably wrongly, either as a minor predecessor to Leibniz or as a follower of More. Unlike many women, she managed to produce and have preserved a substantial work of metaphysics in the mainstream tradition of modernist reason. She criticized well-known philosophers, like Descartes and Hobbes. She pronounced on the general nature of reality. She claimed universality for her views and in no way identified them as partial, feminist, or those of a woman. But even with Conway, the addition of a female voice to the canon involves readjustments.

One point of conflict is the relation between theology and philosophy. Contemporary philosophy prides itself on successful separation from religious contagion, a move that seems necessary if philosophy is to retain academic respectability in a secular age. At the same time, avowed religious motivations and theological sources were common among philosophers in the modern period. Although the references are sloughed off as unimportant in contemporary analytic interpretations, many of the great moderns cite scripture in support of their philosophical conclusions. A notable example is Locke, whose *Treatises of Government* are liberally strewn with biblical quotes and for whom biblical narratives shape ideas of man, woman, and nature. Given the familiarity of biblical motifs, Locke's scriptural gloss can seem expendable, leaving his conclusions to stand alone as common-sense truth. What must immediately strike a contemporary Western reader of Anne Conway's *Principles*, however, are references, not to familiar biblical scripture, but to the non-Christian *Kabbalah Unveiled*. Canonical modern philosophy, whether it acknowledges the fact or not, is European and Christian philosophy, even when philosophers profess skepticism or atheism. At the very origin of modernism, Descartes had no qualms about resting his case on a Christian premise: the idea of an all-powerful, all-knowing, good, and Christian God. It was a statement that could pass as self-evident in Christian Europe, but not necessarily outside of Europe where many sorts of divine principles and forces were worshipped.

Shared Christianity did not ensure consensus. In an age of religious controversy, bloody wars of religion between Christian sects, brutal civil repression of one sect by another, constant expulsion, inquisition, and intolerance were endemic. Religious strife was and continued to be responsible for indiscriminate killing, the devastation of the countryside, and the ruin of economies. In the seventeenth century, virtually all philosophers saw this as a problem for philosophy. A primary job of the philosopher was to search out sources of understanding that could eliminate violence in the name of religion. The great hope for modernist reason was that it might provide such an understanding. If everyone would reason, if irrational religious enthusiasm could be eliminated, there would be no more civil uprisings or religious wars.

But "reason" itself could be defined in competing ways, resulting in renewed controversy. Does reason come prepackaged as dogma in the pronouncements of Church authorities? Can an individual read what is reasonable off Bible verses as it comes direct from God? Is reason attainable by anyone? Is it attainable without the aid of scripture or authority by way of an "inner light" that reveals the truth? Different opinions on the nature and source of reason could result in executions, heresy, ostracism, silencing, and censorship. The answer for some was to give up on religion altogether, and proclaim atheism and instrumental science as the only modern truth. Few were willing to go so far. Descartes's extended matter, with soul and God removed, provides a cold and unfriendly environment. Does the universe just crank on and on to no purpose or aim? And what happens to moral responsibility in such a world?

For Conway and for Van Helmont it was not the Bible, emblem of warring Christian elects, encrusted with sectarian conflict, that offered the best source for potentially unifying principle. They hoped to identify an older, purer tradition common to Western monotheistic religions that might be acceptable not only to Christians but to those of other faiths. In the tradition of Jewish mysticism as expressed in kabbalist writings they saw the possibility of an alternate source of wisdom, less compromised by primitive anthropomorphism and tribal history, more consistent with the new science, less conducive to unthinking enthusiasm. An ancient wisdom transmitted to Moses, not written down, but preserved through the ages by Hebrew scribes, Muslim scholars, and Christian kabbalists, would be the basis for a religious consensus free of divisive superstition.

In the seventeenth century, the problem of reconciling meaning in the universe with mechanistic science was at the forefront of philosophical concern. No unbridgeable gap had yet formed between popular credulous belief in miracles, demons, hell, and millennium apocalypse on the one hand, and specialist secular science along with its philosophical helpmate on the other. It was the responsibility of a philosopher to come to terms with findings in cosmology and physics, as well as with religious controversy. How was one to live in Descartes's universe, a universe that God set in deterministic motion like a clock and left to tick on forever? If there are, as Descartes insisted, souls in addition to dead matter in motion, how are those souls to make any contact with the material world, to affect it in any way? Might not a God so remote from the world simply disappear, taking with him any basis for justice or morality? Does mechanistic science really make sense of the experienced world, which appears to be not dead but alive, full of the spirit that science removes from matter? What can a mind do if it is imprisoned in a hard shell of a body except engage in sterile self-contemplation of its own ideas? How is understanding possible if the human mind is so different from its objects?

For Conway, the translation of kabbalist writings prepared by Rosenroth with her and Van Helmont's assistance and encouragement provided an expanded ancient history for a new modern metaphysics consistent both with the findings of science and with revealed religion. *The Principles of the Most Ancient and Modern Philosophy* would no longer be in conflict. The result, she hoped, would be a philosophy acceptable universally to Jews, Christians, Muslims, and pagans. Ignoring much of the inscrutable allegory and hermetic magic in the kabbalistic writings, Conway referred to what she saw as a core of ancient revealed wisdom consistent with modern science. The physical world is permeated with energy and spirit. There is conservation of spirit and matter as transformations occur in nature. God's creation is continuous and immanent.

Conway's ontology resists classification within the metaphysical categories borrowed from medieval scholasticism. According to those categories, a philosopher can be an Aristotelian pluralist, a monist like Spinoza, a dualist like Descartes, or a materialist like Hobbes. In Conway's view none of these positions reflects reality. Spinoza's pantheism conflates God and the created world. Cartesian dualism creates an unbridgeable split between the spiritual and the material. Aristotelian pluralism imprisons creatures in essence so that change and perfectibility become impossible. Instead Conway posited a trinity of substances: God, Christ, and the whole created universe in which there is no substantial division between mind and body, spirit and matter.

Part of Conway's estrangement from Henry More was due to the unorthodox character of her theology. Her Christ is not the historical, magical, reincarnated Messiah of popular Christian belief, but a spiritual principle that mediates between God and the creature world. Her God is not a fatherly anthropomorphic figure who created the world like a watchmaker makes a watch or a builder a house and then tinkers to keep it in motion. Nor is he a willful heavenly "Lord" issuing tyrannical judgments that send believers to heaven and unbelievers to hell. These elements of popular and doctrinal Christian belief, she believed, had to be left behind if a coherent and non-divisive sense of the natural world was to be regained. A new understanding of Christ as a mediating principle, she hoped, "may not a little conduce to the propagation and furthering of the true faith and Christian religion, among the Jews as well as the Turks, and other Infidel Nations, who do not need to know about or profess belief in a historical figure" (*Principles*, pp. 179–80). The irrational and incomprehensible idea of a trinity of Gods including Christ, said Conway, is "a stone of offense to Jews as well as [Muslims] and other people" (p. 150).

Of primary interest from a contemporary point of view, however, is Conway's conception of the created world, the world of human experience. For Conway the essential feature of the creature world is change. Both time and change are infinite aspects of one universal process of mutability. Again Conway bypassed sectarian conflict. There is no historical moment of God's creation subject to disputed interpretations of Genesis and in conflict with scientific archaeology. God is the constant unchanging source of change. Creation is continual and ongoing in infinite time, a non-absolute time that is a dimension of material changing being. Conway struggled to find precarious middle ground between immanence and remote transcendence. God, she said, "is in a proper and real sense, a Substance or Essence distinct from his Creatures." However, at the same time, "he is not divided, or separated from them; but most strictly and in the highest degree intimately present in them all" (*Principles*, p. 149).

Here Conway came precariously close to pantheism, as identified with the "dangerous" views of Spinoza, considered by many to threaten Christian doctrine. If God is in the world how can God direct history? How can God do miracles? Where is heaven? Worse, if God is in the world, or is the world, is there any God at all? If Conway's attempt to find some compromise between immanence and a distant indifferent God was not completely successful, no other philosopher had solved the problem either. The difficulty was both conceptual and existential. Descartes's God creates the universe and then leaves it to work according to natural law. This, for many, was the necessary premise of any kind of empirical science that assumes regularities in nature. But it also seems to remove Providence from the experienced world, as was often noted by Elisabeth in her letters to Descartes. The key to the difficulty for Conway is change and process. There is no evidence of any beginning or end to change, no final order, no reason to believe in any absolute beginning or end to time. In the material world, there are no fixed entities, either in the sense of fixed species or natural kinds, or in the sense of irreducible atoms out of which everything is made or causal laws that operate uniformly forever. But inherent in change is divine force.

Conway's references to Rosenroth's *Kabbalah* were not meant to stand alone as evidence for these conclusions. Conway drew on observations and rational arguments from the new sciences. She pointed out some of the conceptual problems with the idea of irreducible material atoms. If there are atoms in this sense, she argued, then "all motion would cease" because motion depends on moving parts (*Principles*, p. 163). If at some primary level there are no moving parts, atoms are effectively nothing because action requires plurality. No movement is possible in an indivisible unit because no inner response either to itself or to anything outside it is possible. Such a being could not receive or retain the image of anything (p. 208). Although there may be physical "monads" in what Conway called the first state of the materiality of concrete matter, these material constituents should not be confused with the idea of atoms as irreducible building blocks of matter (p. 163). Commentators would later cite Conway's use of the expression "monad" to prove her influence on Leibniz, but Conway's monads are not Leibniz's windowless preharmonized units. Consistently with twentieth-century physics, Conway's monads have internal complexity and can be broken down into subparticles in an endless process. The irreducible plurality of substance is, Conway argued, the basis for scientific accounts of phenomena in terms of subtler parts as opposed to reliance on mysterious forces and occult powers.

Questions arising from Cartesian dualism were troubling to Conway, as they were to Elisabeth. Given that in Descartes's system the link between mind and body is inexplicable, there is a danger that the mind will disappear, leaving a deterministic clockwork universe, in which free will, moral responsibility, and progress in human affairs are impossible to conceive. The result can be a dangerous schism between increasingly dogmatic, irrational, and militant sectarian religion on the one hand, and atheistic instrumental science producing tools of destruction for all comers. How do the mathematical formulas of science relate to the world as experienced painfully or pleasurably by human beings? Where is meaning or purpose to be found in a mechanical universe? Somehow, it seemed to Conway, spirit and matter had to be brought back together in one coherent metaphysics to vitalize both religion and science.

Conway criticized Cartesian definitions of matter as what is divisible, impenetrable, and mutable, and of spirit as what is indivisible, penetrable, and unchanging. In argument after argument, she showed the artificiality of these distinctions. In fact, bodies are more or less penetrable. All are penetrable by subtler bodies. Even a hard body can be permeated by fire. Spirits in turn are only more or less penetrable. A spirit can become hard, closed off to others, impervious to outside influences, ungiving and obdurate. She urged the return of words to their natural meaning. Spirit is what we call the more penetrable subtle forms of substance; body the more obdurate and hard forms of substance. The Cartesian idea of matter on its own without spirit or energy, said Conway, is of a "non-being," a "false fiction or Chimaera" (*Principles*, p. 197). Physical phenomena cannot be explained in terms of the mechanical movements of such a matter. Mechanical pressure or impact of one particle on another cannot account for motion transmitted through a medium, for refraction, reverberation, or the behavior of light. Mechanism cannot account for organic form, the cohesion of bodies, or action at a distance.

Further disproof of the metaphysical distinction between spirit and matter comes from the close bond between body and mind. Without the assumption that they are one substance, argued Conway, there can be no explanation for the unbreakable cohesion of mind and body, no reason why a soul might not separate from its body, enter another body, leave again, bizarre possibilities that even the sensible Locke was willing to entertain. Why might a soul not tire of its body altogether and float around on its own? Why not wake up some day and find yourself in someone else's body. If dualism is correct, there is no reason why a spirit needs to be encumbered with a body at all.

Conway also cited in support of her critique of dualism the response and love that humans have for the physical world. If the soul is set apart from the material world, why do humans love things? Why do they love animals, landscapes, houses, children, even their own bodies, if these are only bits of matter. We might use the mechanisms found in matter coldly and dispassionately to further our interests, but we would not love, an experience that Conway took as fundamental in human experience. Love of one's mate, for Conway, is not an effect of a bodily mechanism of reproductive instinct but comes from an essential similarity between human creatures, from the fact that they are the same stuff, which explains why human bonds like marriage are unbreakable and not expendable when the instrumental purpose of child-care has been accomplished. Nor can dualism explain our love of animals. For Conway, the created universe—all of reality apart from God and Christ—is one substance, which means there is no essential distinction between animal machines and human bodies with souls. As did many at the time, Conway balked at the counter-intuitive conclusion of Cartesian dualism that animals have no souls. It is obvious, she said, that animals suffer, have sensation, and even think. God made, said Conway, "all Nations, or Armies of Creatures, out of one blood" (*Principles*, p. 178).

If the universe is not Cartesian matter in motion, for Conway, it is not matter imprinted with Aristotelian form either. The problem is not so much that Aristotelian essences are unknowable, she said, as that they are nowhere to be found in nature. There may be "Universal Seeds, and Principles of all Things" but these are no more than the "Springs" and "Fountains" from which the great diversity of living and non-living things are generated and continue to be generated (*Principles*, p. 165). There are species or natural kinds, but given the essential mutability of physical substance, a species is not a straitjacket. Individuals, animal or human, change beyond their apparent species being. A man can become a new kind of man; a horse a better horse. A species, or natural kind, can change enough so as to become another species. Animals, like horses or dogs, have their own perfection and their own potential for change. A horse can become a better runner, a dog a more expert hunter. When an animal dies, changes in that individual may be passed on to its progeny, even to the point where eventually over a period of time a different species of animal evolves. Conway's evolution is due not only to "mechanisms" of chance mutation and natural selection, but to a drive to perfection built into nature. There is no miraculous forming of the first man in an act of separate creation, no afterthought creation of a servant and companion for that man in the shape of Eve, no refusal of evidence that human beings evolved from early primates. God's creation is evolution's tendency toward survival, integration, formal complexity, and consciousness.

Perfectibility and the possibility that a species can evolve in new forms rescue the world from purposeless deterministic mechanism, but created other problems for philosophers like Conway. If the world as a whole is inevitably getting better, how can one explain evil and suffering? This was a particularly difficult question for Conway, who suffered from painful incapacitating migraines. One attraction of the doctrine of the transmigration of souls in Rosenroth's *Kabbalah* was that it seemed to provide a solution. Suffering may seem unmerited, but if transmigration occurs suffering can be linked to evil in a previous life. Suffering can be seen as a source of perfectibility, a way to purge evil and prepare for a better life to come. Conway's own suffering could be seen in that light. Her migraines were an occasion for secluded meditation and conceptual work that she might not have otherwise undertaken. Unlike Leibniz, Conway did not argue on the basis of logical deduction that since God was omnipotent everything happens by necessity, resulting in the best of all possible worlds regardless of appearance. Her theology was descriptive. Evil does occur. The problem becomes how to reconcile evil with a God-created universe. Conway's answer is "indifference of will." Regardless of the drive for betterment inherent in all creatures, human beings can act arbitrarily for the worse. Conway's God is not a separate arranger and designer of pre-established harmony, but, consistently with natural theology, the source of continual but also resistible creation.

The great wealth of natural history observation available in the seventeenth century influenced Locke's moral skepticism. There is hardly any cruelty or barbarism, observed Locke, after reading his travel tales, that men do not practice somewhere on the globe. Natural history inspired another kind of insight for Conway. Everywhere in the natural world there is vibrant transformation, metamorphosis, and change. Environments change. Grass dies out. Creatures adapt and change in order to be able to nourish themselves on other food. Rocks dissolve and become sand. Hybrids and mutations occur. Plant a wheat seed and something like barley sprouts. Animals die, are eaten by men, and animal flesh turns into men's spiritual energy. An animal eats grass; grass turns into animal flesh. A worm spins a larva and turns into a butterfly. There is no justification in Conway's metaphysics for setting men apart from this process of change. A man can sink so low, can become so prey to lust or anger that he is an animal. The species man might sink so low that it is no longer "man." Alternatively, in an evolutionary sense, over successive generations, an animal might turn into a man. Is man so great, she asked? Or is man just part of the "ladder of being"? Some of Conway's examples reflect common misapprehensions of her day, like the spontaneous generation of animals from mud. In spirit they are consistent with contemporary biological science. The organic and the inorganic world is one substance; animate life evolves from inanimate substance although we may not know how that happens.

If God is in the world, if the soul is one with matter, does this mean, in effect, that there is no soul? Conway worked to preserve both the continuity of substance and a realistic non-essential distinction between matter and spirit. The created world is one substance; there is only one reality. Everywhere, that one substance is mixed matter and spirit. Passive inert and active generative principles both operate, as substance is more or less solidified or rarified, more or less inert or in motion. No substance or any part of a substance is purely material or purely spiritual. A thought, for example, is active, but not immaterial. It has a bodily aspect, and must have if it is to be retained. There can be no immaterial inscription on the blank tablet of the mind, or any sorting of insubstantial ideas in a mysterious inner mental space, as the empiricist Locke seemed to suggest. Memory requires matter, requires a mechanism of nerves and neural pathways so that it has permanence, otherwise ideas would immediately disappear. The distinction between mind and body, Conway insisted, is "modal and gradual, not essential or substantial" (Principles, p. 190). A person can be more or less spiritual and more or less bodily; but even when the bodily aspect of a person predominates and she is driven by brute instinct or appetite, a small residue of spirit remains as a source of redemption and rehabilitation.

If soul or spirit or mind is only an aspect of substance and plural as all substance is plural, asks Conway (Principles, p. 210), what sense can be made of the mind as a "central or governing spirit," as a center of consciousness? What happens to unity and indivisibility as the defining feature of spirit? Conway's conception of the mind might be compared to the neural networks of contemporary biology. There is no mystical unity, she argued; all spirit is plural, but there is a center of consciousness in humans and higher animals, a nexus where lines of spirit and sensitivity meet. Spiritual or neural paths leave from that center and come back to it, making it in some sense directive (p. 210). In man, this spiritual center is particularly firm and indestructible, even more so in spiritually evolved individuals. Unlike Leibniz's dominant soul-monad who directs the body, the function of Conway's center of consciousness is integration and coordination.

Conway ends her study with an answer to what she sees as the most likely criticism of her metaphysics: in effect, she is a materialist and no better than Hobbes. Her response is complex. In part, she agrees with Hobbes; all creatures are of one substance and all are subject to change. That the atheist Hobbes said something does not make it false. But from that premise—that there is always a potential for change—she draws a different conclusion. The universal potential for change from concrete material forms to more subtle and spiritual forms means that perfectibility can be inferred: if all is changing then "nothing is so low that it cannot attain to sublimity" (*Principles*, p. 223). Material change proves that the universe is not meaningless mechanism. She agrees with Hobbes that everything but God has a material aspect, but her understanding of materiality is different. For Hobbes and Descartes, matter is defined by the attributes of extension, impenetrability, shape, and motion. Conway's matter is not inert substance put into motion on impact or pressure from other bits of matter. It has its own attributes of energy and life even in inorganic substances, which over long periods of time may evolve into more conscious forms. Again Conway comes close to immanence. God is no magician creating and destroying substances, but a source of "Fertility or Fruitfulness" that operates within substance so that it changes and develops on its own (p. 225). The result is that spiritual "Life" and material shape or "figure" are distinct but not opposites (p. 226). The material shape of a structure or organ is at the same time "an Instrument of Life, without which no Vital Operation can be performed" (p. 226). Mechanical motion from place to place is a manifestation of "Vital Action" (p. 226). The vital function of an eye or a leg is distinguishable from its material form but is also an aspect of that material form.

So Conway's *Principles* ends. As Van Helmont noted, these are "only Writings abruptly and scatteredly, I may add also obscurely, written in a paper book . . . which she never had Opportunity to revise, correct, or perfect" (*Principles*, p. 240). What further conclusions or revisions Conway might have made is hard to know. Her *Principles*, as they stand, can seem anomalous, out of the mainstream of philosophic thought, worthy perhaps only as a footnote or tribute to the friendship of Van Helmont or the loyalty of More, who continued to praise her even after she turned to Quakers and the Kabbalah. It is hard to know whether to include her among rationalists or empiricists. It is hard to know what to do with her references to the Kabbalah. If it is currently fashionable to acknowledge that the science of the period gained much of its impetus from religious conceptions, the religion cited is always Christianity. Although occasionally a nod is given in the direction of medieval Islamic scholarship that preserved the learning of classical Greece and made advances in fields like algebra, Islamic thought has not been included in accounts of the prehistory of modern philosophy. Other than Spinoza, Jewish thought and scholarship also disappeared out of the philosophic mainstream, along with the physical expulsion of Jews from Europe that inspired the teaching taken by Rosenroth as the major source for his *Kabbalah*.

Conway was not the only seventeenth-century philosopher to take an interest in non-Christian sources. Unmentioned in most history books is Leibniz's interest in the Kabbalah and his collaboration with Van Helmont after Conway's death, or in turn Van Helmont's association with Locke. Around Conway as a canonical figure might begin to form a different constellation of historical figures incorporating sources of European thought that transcend the boundaries of European and Christian sectarianism. No longer is a universal Catholic Church defending antiquated knowledge overcome by a secular science based on observation and experimentation. Other forces and ideas are at work, as described in the revisionist historical studies of Francis Yates and Carolyn Merchant. Paracelsus, Giordano Bruno, Isaac Luria, the elder Van Helmont, inspired by spiritualist and alchemical ideas, might be seen to play an important role in overcoming a stultifying Calvinist insistence on original sin, the culpability of Eve, and predestination. Instead of winning a debate between authoritarian Catholicism and rational science, the enlightenment ideal of progress might be understood to emerge from an exhilarating mix of alchemy, experimentation, spiritualism, and non-credulous religious faith of many kinds and origins.

The course of modern philosophy as it is traditionally understood generates a stock set of philosophical problems: is knowledge based on reason or experience? Can you prove that the external world exists? Is there any absolute standard in ethics? A popular choice is the problem of other minds. If the universe of dualism is populated by individual bits of matter some of which are organized into bodies each with a separate soul attached, how do we know that "other minds" are in those bodies? The question is a staple of modern philosophy: a perennial puzzle on which graduate students practice and professional philosophers lecture. Given that the supposed mind or soul cannot be detected by the senses, the presumption that there are other minds must be based on inference: if a body looks like ours, there is probably a soul in there. The inference is clearly speculative and the assumption of non-material substance unscientific. The "concept of mind" must be eliminated or reduced, but in such a way as to make sense of language that continues to refer to minds. Several well-worn alternatives are available. The mind can be understood as a package of behaviors or as an artifact of grammar.

Several centuries of philosophical analysis go into the articulation and variation of this line of thought, driven by the perceived need to drive unscientific spiritualism out of philosophy. But in Conway's metaphysics, the "problem of other minds" does not arise, nor does the concept of mind need to be eliminated. Soul and body, as one substance, are accessible to the physical senses in some forms and not in others. Even when spirit is so subtle as to be invisible, traces of its activity remain in material form, in the expression of a face, in a gesture, in organic structure. One knows that another person is not a robot or a puppet not because of an uncertain infer-ence that there is a soul or mind "inside" a body, but because one observes mobile, changing aspects of body itself.

There are corresponding political implications. In Conway's universe, per-sons are not separate bits of matter with individual souls who inhabit that matter or "own" it in the form of "private" bodies. They are "brothers" of the flesh and in some sense "one body" (Principles, p. 179). In the place of Locke's and Hobbes's competing individuals inevitably in conflict with each other are interacting organisms. "A society of Fellowship among creatures" (p. 209), based on giving and receiving between individuals, has a basis in nature, and does not have to be negotiated at arm's length by hostile parties in a "state of nature" where life is hostile, brutish, and short. In contrast to Leibniz's windowless monads, Conway's creatures are necessarily commun-icative, constantly taking in both substances and images from other creatures, constantly interactive and mutually dependent. Although a person can become spiritually hardened and impenetrable, this is not a natural state of primal individualism and autonomy but an unnatural repression of the natural fact of interrelatedness. In healthy states, the inner plurality of con-sciousness makes communication with others possible and productive.

But a Creature, because it needs the assistance of its Fellow-Creatures, ought to be manifold, that it may receive this assistance; for that which receives something is nourished by the same, and so becomes a part of it, and therefore it is no more one but many, and so many indeed as there are Things received, and yet of a greater multiplicity; therefore there is a certain society of Fellowship among Creatures in giving and receiving, whereby they mutually subsist one by another, so that one cannot live without another; for what Creature in the whole World can be found that hath no need of its Fellow-Creature?

(Principles, pp. 209–10)

Addition of a figure like Conway to the canon of modern philosophy requires some reworking of historical sources and historical problems in philosophy. It can also cause dislocations at the present end of the historical sequence. Once premodern sources of philosophy are construed differently, lines of philosophical thought converge differently into the present. The standard sequence from Cartesian rationalism, to British empiricism, to Kant, leads naturally, after an interlude of romantic protest, to the logical positivism of the 1930s, to the linguistic and analytic philosophies of the postwar period, and to the increasing emphasis on logical semantics at the close of the twentieth century. In the process, philosophy sheds in successive stages theological or metaphysical elements and finds a proper academic niche as the handmaiden and guardian of the sciences and as under-laborer in the fields of computer programming and linguistics. A line of thought from Conway, however, might lead in other directions.

Many of Conway's theological and metaphysical ideas are echoed in Simone Weil's "thinking body" or non-credulous God, and her sense of the redemptive force of pain (Oppression and Liberty; Gravity and Grace). Evelyn Fox Keller's discussion of methods in the biological sciences might find a "god-mother" in Conway's alive and ever-changing nature. Instead of a guiding metaphor of natural law, stand-in for Descartes's ruling transcendent God, Keller's feminist scientists study self-regulating and dynamic systems that are part of a nature that is generative in its own right. Here a scientist's job is neither to collect and collate data nor to penetrate, uncover, dissect, or master nature from the distant perspective of a controlling mind, but to interact creatively and productively in partnership with nature and its capacities (A Feeling for the Organism, Reflections on Gender and Science, Refiguring Life). In postmodern philosophy after Conway, instead of logical semantics with its truth functional logic, the geometry and topology of organic structures might interest philosophers and lead to new insights in metaphysics.

All history is motivated by a desire to understand the past, but the past to be understood is always the past of a present moment. Feminist readings of history are no exception. Feminist philosophers' present interests in reworking the canon of representative philosophers have included providing new political models, redefining concepts of the body, rethinking relations between humans and nature, and facilitating the participation of women in science. The role played by perspectives and interests in the process of canon formation is often disavowed. Historians, including feminist historians, claim that their history is a true history, consistent with the facts and not tailored by political expediency. Only a few are willing to accept a relativism that admits no distinction between history and fiction and that levels all accounts as alternative constructions. But the awareness that one is reworking history from a present perspective does not necessarily entail relativism. From some perspectives it is possible to see only a small distorted segment of reality. Conscious awareness of perspective, itself, can be a source of expanded corrected vision. Analytic histories successively narrowed the field of historical study to those issues and figures considered relevant to philosophy as an academic specialty. Women philosophers, interested in understanding the broader implications of current research in genetics, cosmology, and evolution, might find Conway's speculations worthy of inclusion as one of the sources of modern philosophy.

Further reading

Some early work rediscovering women philosophers was done by Mary Ellen Waithe in her edited volumes *Modern Women Philosophers 1600–1900*. Waithe includes accounts of a number of women philosophers of the modern period, including Conway and Princess Elisabeth.

Rosenroth's *Kabbalah Denudata* was first published in Latin in 1888. An English edition under the title of *The Kabbalah Unveiled* was translated by S. M. Mathers and published in 1968.

The publishing history of Conway's *The Principles of the Most Ancient and Modern Philosophy* is complex. The 1690 version was translated from English into Latin. For an English edition in 1692, a translation was made from the Latin back into English, the original English manuscript apparently having been lost. Two English editions are now available. Loptson's edition includes both the Latin and the English versions and a useful introduction to her life and work. Loptson also includes commentary on the text, which links some of her ideas to those of contemporary philosophers such as Saul Kripke and Alvin Plantinga. The references in this chapter are to the Loptson edition. A more recent edition is also available from Cambridge (1996) edited by Allison Coudert and Taylor Corse, also with an excellent introduction to Conway's life and thought.

Although few of Conway's letters have survived, some are collected in *The Conway Letters: The Correspondence of Anne, Viscountess Conway, Henry More, and Their Friends, 1642–1684*, edited by Marjorie Hope Nicolson. Nicolson also provides information on Conway's life and work.

A detailed account of Conway's circle can be found in Allison Coudert's *The Impact of the Kabbalah in the Seventeenth Century* and *Leibniz and the Kabbalah*. Francis Yates's *The Rosicrucian Enlightenment* broke new ground in reconsidering non-rationalist hermetic, kabbalist, and alchemical sources of scientific revolution in the modern period

For more on Weil and possible new directions in philosophical thought see Nye, *Philosophia: The Thought of Rosa Luxemburg, Simone Weil, and Hannah Arendt*.

5

JEAN JACQUES ROUSSEAU AND THE NOBLE SAVAGE

What is man? What is the characteristic look and behavior of a man? For an upper-class Greek in ancient Athens, the answer was clear. A man was someone like himself, civilized, literate, a city dweller able to manipulate language to persuade or refute, a property owner rich enough to avoid manual labor. Aristotle's metaphysics expressed this conviction in theoretical terms. Man is a "form" or "essence" that imprints more or less clearly on matter. Some individuals—slaves, foreigners, non-Greeks, and of course women—are human but less perfect exemplars. They exhibit some of the form and characteristics of man but not all, especially in respect to the rationality that distinguishes man from other forms of animal life.

Conway's discussion of natural kinds illustrates how far modern scientists and philosophers had moved away from this Aristotelian view of man's essence by the late seventeenth century. In Conway's system, there are no permanent forms in nature. Man is mutable, one of the shapes that substance takes but like all physical things, subject to mutation. For women and non-European men, the difference could be crucial. If there is no proper form of "man," if there is no species-being to which women or any other group can be unfavorably compared, how is inferior status to be measured or proved? In the essentialist way of understanding species, a woman can be found to have fewer of the necessary characteristics of man. If there is no such standard, women, though different from men, might be the mutating form of a more evolved human organism. A woman's lack of interest in adversarial debate could be adaptation that reduces the chance of war or violence. Her intuitive, emotional "non-rational" styles of thought could lead to better tools for survival in peacefully integrated and ecologically conscious communities. The same could be true of native or primitive man. How is his backwardness or inferiority to be judged? By what standard? Without a fixed

84

ideal, European man might be judged a degenerate or unsustainable form of man doomed to extinction. Yes, said Locke, there may be unknown molecular differences between species, but actual human understanding relies on sensory evidence to construct "nominal" essences based on always limited experience. Rousseau took this line of thinking even further. Apes and monkeys, he said, might be men. It was only prejudice not to call them men before some sort of empirical tests are made (*Discourse on Inequality*, p. 81).

A hundred years later, Darwin on the *Beagle*, rounding Cape Horn and observing for the first time the natives of Tierra del Fuego, was still asking the question. What is man? Could these wretched beings observed huddled on the shore, clothed in animal skins, shivering with cold, scavenging for food, be men? Was this an evolutionary throw back to a previous state? A different species altogether? Or had climate change brought about some sort of drastic degeneration? Even by the seventeenth century, Europe was no longer a Christian universe surrounded by inhuman wilderness. It was a small enclave encircled by an enticing and dangerous vastness of peoples and nations different from Europeans in look, habits, thinking. Modern philosophers eagerly read reports of foreign peoples. Accounts came from the Spanish of Aztec empires in Mexico and cannibal Caribs on tropical islands, from Jesuit missionaries in Canada of innocent children of Eden, fierce but perhaps without original sin. As Europeans penetrated to inland areas, African warriors in feather headdresses and Indian princes captured the fancies of readers.

By the eighteenth century there was a crisis in classification for all species. Natural historians struggled to catalogue thousands of specimens of plants and animals that overflowed the curiosity cabinets of European collectors, from South America, China, Africa, and the Indies. Linnaeus proposed a neo-Aristotelian sexual system of classification of plants to replace the old essential characteristics. In 1747, a few years before Rousseau wrote his *Discourse on the Origins of Inequality*, Buffon published *Histoire naturelle*, including evidence that there might be no systematic species categories at all but only degrees of difference. Science was moving closer and closer to Conway's metaphysics, in which there are no fixed organic forms, no intentionally designed kinds, but only an unprogrammed variety of organic structures.

New kinds of humans did not fit easily into a collector's cabinet, but they too were displayed and catalogued. Live specimens were paraded on concert stages; dead, they were pickled and dried for natural history exhibits. Examples of exotic humans were bought for study from the Aleutian Islands, from the north woods of America, from the Cape of Good Hope. Attempts to impose some order on human difference continued. Was there one creation of man? Or two? A botched pre-Adamite creation? And then afterward "man" proper? Or had Adam been the only human ancestor, and had a falling away from type occurred? Linnaeus in his *Systemae Naturae* distinguished four kinds of man with distinctive features: law-governed *Homo europaeus*, opinion-governed *Homo asiaticus*, caprice-governed *Homo africanus*, and custom-governed *Homo americanus*. In the 1770s Blumenbach began a study of human skulls, isolating features that would measure degrees of "degeneration" from type caused by climate or circumstance. Cuvier proposed a three-part classification of Europeans, Caucasians, Mongolians, and Negroes. Charles White pioneered a measure of human degeneration that would become increasingly popular. A degree of "facial angle" he said, along with penis size, marked a gradation from European to Asiatic, to Negroid, and then at the lowest level to orang-utan and monkey.

The sexual habits of savage man were singled out for special attention. Virtually all the modern philosophers, with the exception of Descartes, at one time or another in their writings reported on exotic marital or amatory behavior in "primitive" lands. Tales of Turkish harems haunt Wollstonecraft's critique of Rousseau in the *Vindication of the Rights of Woman*. The manipulative power of women like Sophie, she said, is reminiscent of the "seraglio," where a multitude of wives lower themselves to salacious maneuvers to stimulate the jaded appetite of a common husband (*Vindication*, p. 117). The orientalist idea of polygamy, said Wollstonecraft, "blasts very domestic virtue." Men with harems are enervated by the demands of so many women, and their women have irritable nerves and wild fantasies owing to sexual frustration. Wollstonecraft, like so many of her contemporaries, drew on journals that came from the Cook voyages in the Pacific. Georg and Johann Forster, scientist/artists on Cook's voyages, found evidence, she said, that the more vigorous individual in the sex act produces its own kind, with the result that in polygamy fewer men are sired by sexually exhausted husbands and the unhealthy practice of polygamy perpetuates itself (p. 170). Kant, also a reader of the Cook journals, cited an incident reported by Cook to prove that vanity rules a woman's behavior. A native wife was willing to take a beating from her husband, Cook reported, because it was flattering proof of her husband's jealousy (*Anthropology*, pp. 216–17). The South Seas were also on Hume's mind as he reported on polygamy, polyandry, and temporary marriages between sailors and native women in "Of Polygamy and Divorce" (*Essays*, p. 170). Hume had some good-natured fun with reports of Scythian women warriors who control their men by blinding them, likening such Amazons to Scottish women who marry fools without the "eye of understanding" so as to be the master over them ("Of Love and Marriage," *Essays*). Although Scythians and South Sea islanders may have had Hume's tongue-in-cheek approval, he was less tolerant of other native groups. African natives, he said, are naturally inferior. Africans have no civilization, have invented nothing, have no art and no science. Here, said Hume, nature indeed made an "original distinction" between rational and irrational "breeds of men." If in Jamaica a black is praised as a man of learning, no doubt he is "like a parrot, who speaks a few words plainly" ("Of National Characters," *Essays*, p. 208).

Even in the midst of arguing urbanely that standards of taste vary around the world, and that shock to arrogance and conceit may be all that supports charges of barbarism, Hume could exhibit remarkable prejudice. The Koran, he said, "bestows praise on such instances of treachery, inhumanity, cruelty, revenge, bigotry, as are utterly incompatible with civilized society" ("Standard of Taste," *Essays*, p. 229). Certainly it was a judgment that owed more to romantic tales of Arab atrocity than to careful study of ancient texts. It was travelers' tall tales, not careful study of non-European art, that informed Hume that "the coarsest daubing contains a certain luster of colors and exactness of imitation which are so far beauties, and would affect the mind of a peasant or Indian with the highest admiration" ("Standard of Taste," *Essays*, p. 238). A sophisticated European, with his wider experience, should view such supposed inferior judgments with indulgence, said Hume. He should put himself in the place of the ignorant savage who does not have the advantage of education in the civilized arts (p. 239). Tolerant though he was willing to be, there was little doubt in Hume's mind as to the superiority of European taste, whether it was in art or in marital arrangements.

Locke had a particular interest in native Americans. "In the wild woods and cultivated waste of America left to Nature," he said in his *Treatises*, "without any improvement, tillage, or husbandry, a thousand acres will yield the needy and wretched inhabitants as many conveniences of life as ten acres of equally fertile land does in Devonshire where they are cultivated" (*Treatises*, II, Section 37). Whether or not Indians were another species, whether or not they were a degenerate form of man, whether or not their taste in art was inferior or their women were promiscuous, Indians were not industrious and rational by European standards, said Locke, citing Genesis in support of the right of Europeans to take over their territories. God gave the earth to the industrious and rational, that is to Europeans with their intensive and commodity-driven agriculture and their aggressive appropriation of natural resources.

In *Essay concerning Human Understanding* Locke collected examples of non-European atrocity to prove that there are no innate moral ideas. Infanticide, the exposure of unwanted elders, cannibalism, all were condoned and practiced in foreign nations, reported Locke. "The virtues whereby the Tououpinambos believed they merited paradise, were revenge, and eating abundance of their enemies. The saints who are canonized among the Turks, lead lives which one cannot with modesty relate" (*Essay*, Book I, Chapter iii, Section 7). One of Locke's most shocking examples came from the journals of Garcilaso de la Vega, whom he frequently cited. In Peru, he reported after de la Vega, warrior tribes used captive women as breeding stock, siring children on the women, and then fattening and eating the children, and finally eating the women when they were past child-bearing age (*Treatises* I, Section 57; *Essay*, Book I, Chapter iii, Section 9).

References such as these are seldom noted in philosophy class where Locke's and Rousseau's state of nature is traditionally presented as an imaginative abstraction without material content. But in the seventeenth and eighteenth centuries, the existence of a "state of nature" beyond the confines of Europe was very real. Steadily Europeans were penetrating a non-European world, carrying with them an export version of philosophical "enlightenment." In Europe enlightenment meant rational and tolerant attitudes to religion or even skepticism and atheism; in foreign lands enlightenment was conversion of natives to unthinking Christian ritual and obligatory creeds. In Europe enlightenment meant increased freedom to acquire property; abroad it meant that native lands were given to European plantation owners. Democratic institutions were slowly developing in Europe; outside of Europe traditional institutions of self-government were being supplanted by the dictatorial rule of large trading companies. Advances in production aided by science eased famine in Europe; abroad, conversion of subsistence farming to profit driven commodity production for export caused widespread hunger. Everywhere European power buttressed by the military inventions the new science made possible seemed ascendant. European men, it seemed, were in fact the God-like creatures that Captain Cook claimed the islanders took him to be.

Here Rousseau strikes a new note. Locke might comment that, in comparison to some European practices, "irrational untaught inhabitants" in the

"Woods and Forests" do not do too badly following nature. He did not call the natives "noble" and he was far from ready to give up life in London to live in a "state of nature." Hume might titillate his readers with tales of oriental polygamy and Amazonian matriarchy, but he had no intention of abandoning Parisian salons. Only Rousseau dreamed of escape; only Rousseau judged the savage noble and imagined sharing his life. Only Rousseau would have taken as emblem for his philosophy a transplanted tribesman transported to elegant decadent Paris, forced to mime its strange and incomprehensible behaviors, waiting only for the first opportunity to return to his native land.

For the frontispiece to the 1755 edition of his *Discourse on the Origins of Inequality*, Rousseau chose an illustration commemorating such a return to "nature." The engraving pictures a scene on the beach at the Cape of Good Hope at the southern tip of Africa, site of the triumphant breakthrough of Europeans to direct trade with the East. In the foreground of the illustration a scantily dressed figure in a fur loincloth cringes back and away from a group of Dutch burghers elaborately dressed in suits, lace collars, and plumed hats. The man is a "Hottentot," Rousseau made clear in his explanatory note, using the derogatory term current among Dutch colonists for Cape natives. The Dutch look down on him with various expressions of surprise and incredulity. Behind them rise the defensive turrets of a castle or fort. Beyond stretches the open sea on which floats a flotilla of large sailing ships. The Dutch are puzzled and questioning. They have trouble understanding what the native thinks he is doing. Where is he going? And why has he laid the bundle of Western clothes down at their feet? Why has he put back on native dress?

Rousseau explained the real-life incident the engraving commemorates. The governor of the Dutch colony at the Cape undertook to civilize a Cape native. He took the man from childhood, educated him, and gave him employment in Europe. After some years, he brought him back to the Cape for a visit. The man visited his relatives inland, then returned to the Fort, laid his European clothes in a bundle at the governor's feet, and vowed the governor would never see him again. The moral as Rousseau saw it was clear: the savage state is the happier state. Only by coercion or chance would anyone leave it for European civilization (*Discourse*, pp. 48, 92–3). Europeans will not succeed in "civilizing" natives or in overcoming their natural repugnance for European ways. A savage brought to Europe may "admire"; he will never "covet" the uncomfortable clothes, the heavy weapons, the sciences, or the pretenses of Europeans.

Illustrations are not regularly reprinted in philosophy texts, nor is Rousseau's explanation for the engraving that introduces his social philosophy included in excerpts from the *Discourse*. For the purposes of analytic interpretations, Rousseau's views on "Hottentots" can conveniently be forgotten. Feminist philosophers, however, sensitized to differences in perspective and claims by women of color, took such images and metaphors seriously. In the 1970s and 1980s a new wave of feminist activism had been split by controversy. Charging that feminism was dominated by one kind of woman—white, of European descent, heterosexual, and middle-class—women of color and lesbian women defected. Anxious and troubled soul-searching and rethinking resulted in a new consciousness of ways in which gender and race are intertwined. Previous feminist social thought had tended to follow European models. Feminist political theories were variants of either the liberal egalitarianism of democratic theorists like Locke or the radical socialism of Marx. Both, claimed women of color, assumed European perspectives and harbored tacit racism. White feminists might interpret social theory from the perspective of a white woman's claim to Locke's natural rights of man, or from the perspective of a white woman worker's rights, but theory could look very different from the perspective of women who formed along with non-European men an underclass of domestic workers in Europe and North America, and a "third world" of impoverished postcolonial subjects abroad.

Throughout the 1980s and 1990s, theories of "difference" were generated by women of color, women of mixed descent, and white women interested in colonial studies. Many feminists repositioned themselves "at the margin" between a Eurocentric West and subjugated others. Inevitably the interest in non-Western perspectives was extended to the history of philosophy. From the perspective of American Indians dispossessed of their lands, Locke's defense of property rights was seen as transparently self-serving. From the perspective of Africans or Caribbeans, Hume's pronouncements on "experienced" as opposed to "primitive" standards of taste in art revealed submerged prejudice in aesthetics. Insights such as this were important both practically and theoretically. If the women's movement was to survive, some degree of solidarity between different women had to be regained, including a shared sense of history. For women of color, that history would have to include understanding of the ways philosophy had assumed, rationalized, and at times promoted racial and cultural inequality. This interest in how ethnicity might shape philosophical theory was not only politically expedient;

there was a growing sense that a deeper understanding of texts was possible when texts were interpreted from postcolonial and minority standpoints.

As a theorist of difference, Linda Zerilli in *Signifying Woman* pointed out similarities between the native in Rousseau's frontispiece and the "signifier" woman. If the Hottentot cannot be made a "man" in the European sense of man, neither can a woman. Both are "other," both are different, both are what the man is not—not mind but body, not rational but passionate. Overcome by emotion at seeing his relatives again, the Cape native irrationally abandons the advantages the governor has offered to him. They cannot be his and he knows it. As Zerilli put it, "citizen" in modernist political theory is defined by excluding what a citizen is not, and a citizen is not "woman" and not "native," which shows why neither natives nor women can be simply added on as citizens in modern Western nation states. Both are "other," both are the "not-man" that is the contrast that defines "citizen man."

Zerilli relied heavily on post-Saussurean discourse theory to show the importance of language in "constructing" such meanings as "man" and "citizen," and ultimately in constructing political reality. Orthodox non-feminist political theory, said Zerilli, gives "an illusion of mimesis," but rather than describe reality, it lays out the terms for political debate. Rousseau in his account of savage origins weaves "a story out of historical events that only appear to have an intrinsic meaning" (*Signifying Woman*, p. 4). Zerilli, like many feminists inspired by the "French feminism" of the 1980s and 1990s, embraced the structuralist/poststructuralist thesis that meaning is internal to language, not established by reference to non-linguistic objects or events, but created in intralinguistic relations between concepts. On this view, the meaning of "savage," "native," or "woman" is not ostensively anchored to physical or historical fact, but is a result of patterns of oppositions that "map" meaning within a language and make logical inference possible.

Zerilli also embraced equally popular feminist "deconstruction" techniques, borrowed from the French philosopher Jacques Derrida. Constructed meanings are not perfectly ordered. The ambiguity and contradiction in concepts of "woman" and "native" allow what she calls a "feminist intervention" in what otherwise might seem to be a closed system of conceptual relations. Inconsistencies in political theories like Rousseau's are not simply mistakes in logic, but the inevitable shifting of "metaphors" that create meaning and underlie surface logic. Especially the "metaphor" of woman, said Zerilli, signifies a breakdown in meaning, a kind of "abyss." Rousseau's woman—

consoling/frightening, dangerous/reassuring, mother/witch—is the "figure" of that breakdown and an emblem of the chaos that attends social change.

Returning to Rousseau's Hottentot after a rich mix of Lacanian psycho-analysis, Derridean deconstruction, and Kristevan semiotics, Zerilli linked Rousseau's tribesman to the rejection of the feminine. The Hottentot, she said, is an image in a "fully imaginary journey" undertaken by Rousseau and more generally by European man to return to his childhood and recover the voice of the "mother." In approved deconstructive style, she focused on small, seemingly unimportant details to bring out what she saw as coded meanings in Rousseau's illustration. Why, asked Zerilli, does the Hottentot hand back the European shirt and trousers, but keep the cutlass and the necklace? The native is returning to nature, or the primal mother, says Zerilli. He abandons the vanity of the courtier for useful rustic clothing, but like Rousseau he is not willing to give up the possibility of return to European manhood. Rousseau, the noble savage, transported to wicked Paris, dressed up like a fop, leaves civilization for a rustic country retreat, but retains his escape route back to civilization and manly citizenship.

Feminist discourse theory shed new light on texts like Rousseau's, but at a cost. In extreme versions, discourse theory could make it seem that the conceptual structure of European languages, with built-in racial or gender hierarchies, is a prison from which there is no escape. Deconstruction of "patriarchal" or "ethnocentric" images and metaphors could make it seem that the only effective weapon against racism or sexism is academic theorizing that makes little impact on women's or native people's material condition. Even as the textuality of racial or gender concepts is mapped and the fragility of racial and gender oppositions like native/civilized, feminine/masculine is exposed, concrete women and natives continue to suffer.

But Rousseau's "Hottentot" was not a textual abstraction. He was a fact. Vasco da Gama, rounding the Cape for the first time in 1497, was the first reported European, but by no means the last, to capture a Cape native, take him to the ship for observation, and dress him up in European clothes. There were real material purposes behind such experiments. Desperate for fresh supplies for his scurvy-ridden men, da Gama hoped that when the native was put back on shore dressed up in European clothes, the other natives would be impressed. They would gather around and be willing to trade for supplies. They would tell da Gama about jewels, gold, and spices that would make fortunes for him and his Portuguese sponsors. Centuries later, more elaborate experiments with native people were tried. In 1810, a young

Khoikhoi woman, known as the Hottentot maiden, was brought for display to England. Naked, she was made to walk before audiences so they could marvel at her large genitals and protruding buttocks. After her death, Napoleon's surgeon made a plaster cast of her body, and put it along with some of her preserved body parts on display in the Musée de l'homme in Paris. Whatever abysses of meaning the conflicted Rousseau might have drawn from his Hottentot image, the noble savage was not a figment of his imagination.

Throughout the Discourse, Rousseau refers to published journals and reports from explorers, missionaries, and travelers. The savage is physically strong and not threatened by wild beasts (Caribs in Venezuela, Discourse, p. 22). Savages have keen senses and can smell as well as dogs. They can smell Europeans coming before they are within eyesight (Indians in the Americas, p. 25). Natives can see as well as the Dutch with their spyglasses (Hottentots at the Cape, p. 25). Natives have instinctive customary skills, like fishing, swimming, hunting, and running, but are not inventive (Cape natives and islanders in the Antilles, pp. 21, 72). Native wants are primitive: "Savage man when he has eaten, is at Peace with all Nature, and the friend of all his fellows" (South American Indians, pp. 26, 75). Natives live by instinct, have no foresight, and reason only when pressed by a threatening change of circumstances (Caribs, p. 28). The savage does not fall in love; for this a European appreciation of beauty or moral merit is necessary, but without love he does not suffer from jealousy, and the sexual instinct is not perverted as it is in high society in Paris. Among natives there are no "brutal and depraved tastes," no abortion, imasculati, forced marriages, rape, or prostitution (p. 77). Natural man has no craving for status and display. He values freedom above all. "Entirely naked savages scorn European voluptuousness and endure hunger, fire, the sword, and death to preserve their independence" (p. 57). In place of driving ambition and competition, savage life is one of repose. Striving for status is "horrible" to a savage, who lives within himself and not to impress others.

In Rousseau's version of prehistory, at the most savage edge of humanity, native man wanders the woods without company. Native woman stays with her offspring only for the short time they need her to survive. By the modern period, said Rousseau, native peoples outside of Europe have made a further step. They live in settled villages and families. They enjoy simple communal life. They know the joys of marriage and domesticity. They observe rudimentary property rights. They engage in uncoerced cooperative activities like dancing and telling stories around the campfire. In rustic huts, decorated with feathers, shells, and tattoos in festive fashion, natives entertain themselves with simple handmade musical instruments on idyllic South Sea islands, free, healthy, peaceful, sexually expressive, everything that cold, damp, violent, prejudiced Europe is not. No one, said Rousseau, expressing the moral that the illustration in the Discourse depicts in graphic images, no one would leave such a happy state except by fatal accident (Discourse, pp. 48, 92–3). Europeans might capture, corral, induce a native to leave his home, but they would never convert the noble savage or overcome his "repugnance" to Western ways. The "Hottentot" will always resist. Dressed up in uncomfortable Western clothes, educated, taught to pass as civilized; when given the chance he will return to his "state of nature."

In Emile, when Rousseau decides on the one book to be given to his ideal pupil Emile, he chooses Defoe's fictional tale of the slave trader Robinson Crusoe, shipwrecked on a desert island, forced to become a natural man and as a consequence to see Europe in different terms. For Sophie, Emile's ideal mate, he chooses another fictional travel tale, set in ancient Greece, Fénelon's epic of an imaginary voyage by Telemachus in which Telemachus encounters Greek islanders very much like North American Hurons in dress and habits.

Rousseau, like Hume and Locke, and later Kant, was an armchair traveler. His perceptions were necessarily partial and second hand. He did not see the virtual extermination of the native peoples in the Caribbean by disease and violence, the ruthless foraging along the Orinoco River for miraculous cures for European ills, the expulsion of North American Indians off fertile lands, the destruction of Khoikhoi culture by the Dutch at the Cape of Good Hope. But he came closer than other philosophers to the prophetic sense of a comparison that did not always favor the West. Something in the great ascendancy of modern enlightened Europe had gone wrong; some ingredient of human happiness was lost in this great civilization fated to dominate the globe. As Rousseau absorbed Jesuit reports from Canada, Dutch missionaries' letters home from the Cape, Spanish journals of conquest in the Caribbean, a dream image formed of another life. In the place of an inevitable quarreling over riches and status, might there be a sense of community? Instead of Hobbes's unfeeling calculated self-interest, might there be spontaneous unmediated feeling? Instead of Kant's repressive sexual ethics, might there be free expression of passion? Instead of logic and erudite theory, intuitive wisdom? Instead of hypocritical outward piety, natural virtue?

In fact, of course, beyond Europe there was no one noble savage or state of nature that could validate that dream image. The non-European world was infinitely diverse: ancient Chinese high culture, Muslim theocracy, village communities ruled by councils of elders, island seafaring nations. Although many cultures were already distorted and decimated by the European advance, all retained some of their own history and values. Soon ethnographers and anthropologists would struggle to find examples of native peoples uncorrupted by Europe, and then struggle even harder to understand those peoples in terms that did not import their own biases and preconceptions. Rousseau's ambivalence would remain, along with his yearning for a simpler more natural form of life. Were Western men and women to go back to the woods? Go native? Rousseau in his fictional accounts of Emile and Julie in *La Nouvelle Héloïse* showed the futility of such a step. A European man and his woman could find a rustic retreat, but they could not insulate themselves from the world around them or from their own destructive feelings, no matter how remote their "desert." In the end Rousseau's heroes and heroines do not prosper. Emile becomes a slave. Sophie dies. Julie finds no happiness in life.

What has all this to do with philosophy? What has it to do with the main tenets of Rousseau's social theory, with the social contract, the "general will," with the "philosophical content" of Rousseau's writing? Is Rousseau's fascination with the noble savage relevant to the logical conclusion of the *Discourse* that a social contract is necessary to establish the legitimacy of governmental authority, given the natural freedom of man? Is the Hottentot maiden relevant to a comparison between direct democracy as Rousseau conceived it and Locke's representative democracy? Why not leave out local color and simply say that Rousseau's state of nature reflects a more optimistic view of human nature than either Locke's or Hobbes's, which in turn influences his more communitarian construction of civil society. Analytic readings of Rousseau and other modern philosophers sloughed off references to foreign cultures and travelers' tales as extraneous to these lines of argument, the lines of argument that figure in contemporary philosophical debates.

For women of color, postcolonial women, and white feminists aware of the historical associations between racism and sexism, references to the Americas and other non-European territories were more difficult to ignore. The submerged premise on which Hume's theory of taste depends—that Europeans are more experienced observers—privileges European art and justifies the destruction of non-European traditions. Locke's state of nature supports a legal tradition that upheld the appropriation of Indian land in the

Americas. Bypassing preformed issues and problems, and variations in surface logic, feminist readings "from the margins" developed a new style of
philosophical interpretation of texts like Rousseau's. Beneath the customary
logic, shaping the concepts on which philosophical arguments are based,
were pictures and stories that had been and are taken for granted and not
critically examined. On this view, philosophy is not words on a page or arguments to be followed, but flesh and blood: Catholic conquistadors claiming
Aztec empires for Spain, colonists in the new world encroaching on Indian
land, Dutch settlers at the Cape displacing the native tribes, European art connoisseurs examining native masks with good-humored indulgence.

What is happening to philosophy here? The selective process at work in
analytic treatment of texts tends to single out a core of doctrine and cast off
extraneous references. A sharp distinction is made between fiction and non-
fiction, theory and history, argument and description. But feminist attention
to Rousseau's historical references to Hottentots and Caribs gives concrete
material meaning to concepts like the "golden age" or "state of nature" or
"noble savage." Rousseau's philosophy becomes the philosophy of a particular man, a vagabond in Paris, new possibilities for human life impinging on
his consciousness at every turn of the page of a natural history book, in
every twist of plot in romantic travel tales of fierce tribes, in every idyllic
description of tropical paradise. It is the philosophy of a man in sexual con-
fusion, immature in his emotions, motherless, yearning for tenderness,
shocked at woman's new boldness in sex, incapable of the cold-blooded calculation necessary to succeed in eighteenth-century France, longing for
escape from his own frustrations.

Seen in this context even Rousseau's most "philosophical" text, The Social
Contract, the text most often assigned in philosophy class, gains new meaning. In her classic study of Rousseau's social contract theory, Judith Shklar
focused on Men and Citizens rather than theories and arguments. Rousseau's
social contract, she said, could be understood not as an ingenious solution
to a logical puzzle—how it is possible for a man to retain his freedom and
yet be subject to governmental authority—but as an emotionally fraught and
inevitably failed and tragic attempt to reconcile two incompatible demands:
the demand for "savage" freedom and the demand for safety in a modern
world of ever-increasing domestic and global inequality. To meet those
demands, said Shklar, Rousseau spliced together two historical/literary
images. On one hand, Rousseau's ideal republic preserves Homer's image of
the private household, ruled by an autonomous manly warlord. Here

domestic virtues are willingly observed, the dangerous power of women is overcome, and man is safe from the siren call of sophisticated city life. Superimposed is Plato's dream of an ordered and public-spirited Spartan state in which individual interests are suspended in favor of general welfare. In some unfathomable fashion, Rousseau's citizen man must find a way to go from one to the other, from the nostalgic country retreat where wife and servants cater to his needs, to the assembly where he thinks only of the good of the community.

With such readings come new standards of evaluation. The problem with Rousseau's politics is not that it is logically inconsistent, or even that it is unrealizable, both freely admitted by Rousseau himself. As a map of the real and imaginary world as Rousseau experienced it, the weakness is not in inconsistency but in Rousseau's failure to see beyond his own obsessions. When women are in question, it is his women—women as he needs them and wants them to be. With the "Hottentot," it is his noble savage he admires—savages with the kind of freedom and simplicity he longs for. Here feminist theories of difference devised by women of color can be corrective. Rousseau recognizes difference and values difference, but on his own terms. What he does not see, and cannot see, is that those who are different, are not just different, they see their difference differently and they see difference differently. Rousseau may idolize mothers and housewives; he cannot put himself in a woman's situation. He may admire the "Hottentot's" refusal to live as a European; he cannot see the choice with native eyes.

Rousseau gave readers himself, including his weaknesses and his ambivalences. Without pretense and with a frankness often embarrassing, he held nothing back. The world is the world as he lived, felt, and imagined it. When he writes about women, they are his women, women as they treat him, as they disappoint or reward him, women as he would want them to be and fears that they will not be. When he writes about savages, they are his savages, his savage self, the self he would like to have been if he could only free himself of the corruptions of civilized Europe. Woman, savage, even nature itself, are figures acting out his longings and fears. Women are treacherous and immoral; they also metamorphize into angels of the house. Savages are without obligation, appetite-driven, promiscuous, and solitary; on some fragile middle ground between savagery and civilized corruption, they are also "noble."

A personal and romantic style like Rousseau's can be a welcome change from *Treatises* and *Principles*. For many modern philosophers, knowledge is attained by pulling back from the world, putting aside passion and desire for an artificially cool and intellectual grasp of clear and distinct ideas. As with Descartes's wax, the fragrance, the feel, the color of the world disappears, replaced by propositions and geometric proofs. Rousseau represents another style of philosophizing not so cleanly detached from literary traditions, expressive and directly concerned with the living of modern life, conscious of positioning in a wider world of diverse ideas.

If feminists did not find an ally in Rousseau, the problem is not Rousseau's retention of color, emotion, and material reference, or even his negative view of women and women's education. It is his blindness to the fact that the others whose existence he acknowledges—women, Caribs, "Hotten-tots," Indians—have their own view of him. If Rousseau's natural man has a primal aversion to seeing others suffer, he lacks the ability to see the world through the sufferer's own eyes. At home his needs govern. As a public citi-zen he adheres to a "general will" that puts all perspective aside, including his own. Blindly subject to a reason that owes more to totalitarian consis-tency than to harmony between diverse interests, he can only dream an unrealizable ideal republic and an imagined Edenic retreat.

Further reading

Rousseau's engraving and notes are reprinted in the University of New England's edition of his *Discourse on the Origins of Inequality*.

A representative sample of eighteenth-century women's reactions to Rousseau is collected by Mary Seidman Trouille in *Sexual Politics in the Enlighten-ment: Women Writers Read Rousseau*. Trouille includes commentary critical of Rousseau and also commentary that applauds Rousseau for his ideal of domesticity and his interest in women's role in the family. For an extended feminist critical treatment of Rousseau in the context of modern social theory, see Part III of Okin's *Women in Western Political Thought*. Another critical treatment of Rousseau can be found in Elshtain's *Public Man, Private Woman*.

Edward Dudley and Maximillian Novak's collection *The Wild Man Within* examines a wide range of views of the primitive or savage in modern thought. More specifically, see Bernard Smith's *Imagining the Pacific* for an account of how eighteenth-century travel tales influenced ideas of man.

6

DAVID HUME

A friend from the past

If anyone has won the laurel as the contemporary feminist's friend from the past it has been David Hume. Feminists have taken a lively interest in Hume for a variety of reasons. Hume's naming of sentiment as the basis for ethics has been used to support contemporary feminist ethics of care. He has been praised for a non-essentialist social view of personhood that allows women and natives to be included (Sarah Merrill, "A Feminist Use of Hume's Moral Ontology" in Bar On (ed.), *Modern Engendering*). Hume has been applauded for coming up with a woman-friendly way to think about truth (Genevieve Lloyd in "Hume and the Passion for Truth" in Jacobson (ed.), *Feminist Interpretations of David Hume*). Even Hume's biases as they surface in aesthetic or moral theory have been recommended as a useful "caution," a way to separate out what is false or true in feminist ethical theory (Marcia Lind, "Indians, Savages, Peasants, and Women" in Bar On (ed.), *Modern Engendering*). But the most sustained and thoroughgoing presentation and defense of Hume as feminist's friend comes from Annette Baier. In articles and books over a period of decades Baier worked with Hume, weaving her views and his together in a unique style of historical collaboration.

Hume, the radical skeptic, is a staple in the teaching of modern philosophy. His arguments on the failure of reason in the first book of his *Treatise of Human Nature* are legendary and pivotal in the dramatic plotting of the history of modern philosophy. Like Descartes's dreaming argument, Hume's exposure of the fallacy in basing belief on reason is a standard test for the fledging philosopher, challenging her or him to take a step beyond common sense to appreciate the force of Hume's counter-intuitive skepticism. At a more advanced level, students try to devise answers to that skepticism that preserve knowledge and defend truth.

Baier's Hume was different. Charging that many of her colleagues had read selectively, Baier insisted that Book I of Hume's *Treatise*, the book from which readings are usually taken, must be read with the remaining Books II and III on the passions and on morals. Book I, in which Hume argues that the only basis for belief is custom and sentiment, she said, should be understood in the context of the more constructive approach to philosophy in the later books. In turn, the entire *Treatise* should be read with Hume's later essays and histories, materials that philosophers often ignore as of little philosophical interest. The extreme skepticism with which Book I of the *Treatise* ends, argued Baier, is only a temporary resting place. From there Hume goes on to initiate a new "carefree" style of philosophizing and a new non-dogmatic naturalized approach to knowledge. Furthermore, Baier argued convincingly, feminists can learn from Hume's approach to knowledge. The answer to the question posed in the title of Baier's best-known essay on the subject, "Hume: The Reflective Woman's Epistemologist?" is "Yes. He is."

In the introduction to a major book on Hume, *A Progress of Sentiments*, Baier addressed a question on many feminists' minds. Given that the history of philosophy, and the history of modern philosophy in particular, is riddled with misogyny and includes very little writing by women and no writing by any man who is not a white man of European descent, is it a lost cause to attempt to intervene in that history? After proper critiques are made as to the sexism, racism, classism of philosophy, is the logical next step to forget about philosophy as we know it and attempt to reconstruct feminist thought from "reflective women's" own experience. This, some feminists argued, was the only way in which feminist philosophy could escape contamination from concepts based on the nature of man or men's position in modern society. It was an argument that Baier rejected. There are many themes, she argued, in current feminist epistemology that can be found in Hume. Why not "get helpful support from a well-meaning fellow worker, dead or alive, woman or man?" ("Hume: the Reflective Woman's Epistemologist" in *Postures*, p. 20). It is "self-defeating," said Baier, to dismiss all male philosophers without examining each text to see if there might be something of value. Examining Hume, she found much of value.

Baier went on to make an even more controversial claim. Hume, she said, might be taken to be, if not feminine, in a "feminine position." As a "backward" Scot, as someone trying to break into a prejudiced academic establishment without success, Hume is a "suitable mascot for feminist philosophers" (*Postures*, p. 20). Hume was, she said, whether he knew it or not, a "virtual woman" (p. 22), which accounted for his popularity with women and his obvious liking for their company. An "outsider" status shared with women allowed him to conceive "radical goals for the transformation of philosophy" (p. 22). His attack on the sovereignty of reason was, in effect, an attack on the whole "patriarchal tradition" with its assertion of manly reason over feminine passion, appetite, and good sense.

Baier explained how she had come to this conclusion. Educated in Oxford in the 1950s in the heart of the English-speaking philosophical establishment, she was steeped in the standard philosophical wisdom that reason has authority over the common man's feelings, customs, traditions, and habits. The philosopher analyzed, defined, and constructed arguments. Philosophers, both past and present, formulated general laws, which could be applied in morals as well as in natural science. Her first doubts came reading Wittgenstein's *Investigations* with the Oxford philosopher Elizabeth Anscombe. Wittgenstein's meandering but incisive questioning, she realized, undermined the whole program of philosophy as contemporary philosophers understood it. If there are no natural kinds, no inner objects or thoughts, no rigid definitions, no general rules independent of variable "forms of life," what becomes of philosophy? What is the job of a philosopher if it is not, as Wittgenstein seemed to suggest, to give up philosophizing altogether? British and American philosophers responded in various ways to the challenge. Wittgenstein could be downgraded as a crank and ignored, and a program of logical analysis renewed. Some like John Austin, also at Oxford, invented new forms of linguistic analysis based on the "ordinary" use of words that circumvented Wittgensteinian critiques. Baier turned to Hume. For her Hume provided a model for a post-Wittgenstein philosophizing that is not a rigidly ordered academic specialty with dubious roots, but a human endeavor that gives importance to sentimental and social sources of knowledge. She and Hume, it seemed to her, had a common aim: finding a way to think reflectively about human life without relying on dubious faith in the sovereignty of reason.

To discredit Hume and all other male philosophers, Baier suggested, is an epistemological mistake and based on a false view of the mind. The mind is seen as a reflecting mirror, a mirror whose own imperfections may distort reality, but that nevertheless can be polished or adjusted so as to give a relatively clear view of the objects it reflects. If this false view of the mind motivates feminist attempts to go it alone, to think about reality from a woman's own independent reflecting mind, such attempts are bound to fail. Thinking is not a result of any pristine seeing but comes in trains of thoughts always shared with others. Although in theory Hume postulates "simple impressions" he also makes clear they do not figure in human thinking in that state. Thought is never purely private and introspective, but is embedded in tools, material culture, geography, and history. This accounts for Hume's turn from academic analysis to essays on human issues. Feminists who reject the history of thought, who propose going it alone, make a mistake about the mind's autonomy. It is impossible to go it alone, to think free of tradition, said Baier; what is important is to use tradition critically, to pick and choose among the past what best suits feminist sentiments and intuitions. In such a process, said Baier, Hume, whatever his masculine shortcomings, is an ally.

Unlike philosophers who hold an illusory view of the mind as understandable in terms of discrete mental objects such as propositions and representations, Hume, said Baier, was acutely aware how meaning is governed by custom in the form of a public language that mediates experience and ideas. Meaning in language is governed socially and never autonomously, an insight that was also at the heart of the later "linguistic turn" initiated by Wittgenstein. Wittgenstein's arguments against the possibility of a "private language" in which words refer to ideas were aimed at Locke and Descartes with their assumption of mental independence. If meanings are determined socially, there can be "no pretense of building up a public world from subjective pre-social certainties of the sort Descartes seemed to be searching for" (*Progress of Sentiments*, p. 33). In other words, there is no starting afresh from clear and distinct feminist impressions and ideas, and then constructing a feminist theory free of masculine bias.

Again Baier asked the question that comes up over and over in the upheaval of social and intellectual systems taking place in the modern period: What is man? What is man's proper function and role? What is human understanding? What is the human mind? For Descartes the mind is a thing apart, a separate substance set off from the physical world, pre-imprinted with ideas that reflect reality and that are the basis for knowledge. With Locke that imprinting fails. The mind is a thing apart from material life, but it is equipped only with limited ideas from a particular man's or woman's experiences. The link between the spiritual substance or space of the mind and physical bodies weakens. No sure inference can now be made that external things exist as they are conceived by the mind. All people can do is put their ideas in order and hope that something like those ideas probably caused them.

In the concluding sections of Book I of Hume's *Treatise* the basis of even that probable assumption is undermined. Reason utterly fails to prove that there are causes operating in the world, that the future will be like the past, that substances outside the mind exist, or that primary qualities exist in objects anymore than secondary qualities. Reason utterly fails to prove that God or the soul exists, or that anything of the mind exists except an ephemeral stream of consciousness. We continue to believe these things because we cannot help ourselves. We cannot know that they are true. Even mathematics and logic, which seem to depend on pure reason, are uncertain, as the mind must successively doubt whether it has correctly applied formal rules, and with each new doubt compound the probability of having made a mistake. Even here reason leads, when pursued, to "a total extinction of belief and evidence" and a total suspension of judgment (*Treatise*, I, IV, Section 1, p. 183). Our salvation, according to Hume, is weariness. Eventually we lose the impulse to continue a questioning so "tortured" and "unnatural," and return to ordinary belief. Regardless of the pretensions of logicians and philosophers, belief is a product of sentiment and custom. We believe what is our and others' habit to believe. We believe in ideas to which imagination and sentiment give liveliness and vibrancy.

Hume made clear that the greater part of human thinking was "animal intelligence," instinctive, emotional, habit-bound. What makes human thought unique is not the autonomy of a mind standing apart from material or social life with untouched ideas, or even with ideas borrowed from others. It is the more humble human capacity to respond to what others say. Baier titled a series of her lectures, *The Commons of the Mind*. Thinking for Hume and for many feminists, she argued, is not a private activity occasionally shared with others, but a conversation with others, which, for short periods of time, can go on in one's own mind. Instead of private minds locked in personal soliloquy, mind is something we have in common with others.

This Hume recognized and practiced, said Baier. In strategic despair at the end of Book I of the *Treatise*, certain that philosophers and metaphysicians will condemn him, Hume redirects his thinking in Books II and III to a different audience. Said Baier, others should follow his example. It was not so much the failure of Promethean knowledge claims that drove Hume to despair at the end of Book I. Rather it was the understanding that he would be unable to communicate his radical ideas to an academic establishment not interested in change. Ideas are nothing, said Baier along with Hume, unless one can communicate them, unless one can hear and digest others' comments and criticisms. "Response," not logical acuity, is the key to successful philosophy and successful knowledge. For Hume, failure to gain an audience was not only a blow to vanity; it was a blow to truth. "The moral of the story, as I am telling it," said Baier along with Hume, is that "*all our interpretations will 'loosen and fall of themselves' until they become cooperative and mutually corrective*" (*Progress of Sentiments*, p. ix). She called on coworkers and colleagues, feminists and non-feminists, to take up with her the work of reworking naturalized epistemology in a Humean mode.

The mind according to Baier's Hume is an embodied living mind, not radically different in kind from the mind of any other animal. The shift in emphasis from Locke to Hume has been noted by many commentators. In Locke the mind actively sorts, stores, abstracts from its ideas. Hume describes what goes on in the mind naturally and inevitably. The question of where ideas in the mind come from recedes as an issue. They are there. There is no more imprinting by God, or any argument to show that external objects must cause sensations. The undecidable question of whether ideas are caused by external objects, the mind itself, or by God, says Hume, is not "material to our present purpose." We draw "inferences from the coherence of our perceptions, whether they be true or false; whether they represent nature justly, or be mere illusion of the senses" (*Treatise*, I, II, Section v, p. 84). The difference for Hume between ideas that we believe and ideas we do not, or between memory images and imagined images, is internal, in the "vivacity" or "force" with which we conceive ideas. Moving by cause and effect reasoning beyond present impressions and ideas to external objects or historical events is equally due to a natural process, useful for self-preservation and the avoidance of pain. Custom and imagination transfer vivacity from a present impression to ideas when similar ideas and impressions have been in constant conjunction in the past. Given these processes, most of people's beliefs are due to education, which by simple repetition gives vivacity and habit to any idea. All probable reasoning—for Hume virtually all reasoning is probable—is a "species of sensation" (*Treatise*, I, III, Section viii, p. 103). Hume, said Baier, points to passion and morals to drive his point home. To base reasoning on custom and habit may seem strange, until you understand the close connection between belief and emotion and will. If it were only present sensations that arouse emotion and activate the will, we could not foresee danger. If all our ideas excited passion, we would be driven mad. The mental processes of belief formation and cause and effect reasoning are devised by "nature" as a middle ground, so that relatively clear dangers can be avoided and remote possibilities and idle fantasies ignored.

Even in this protective function Humean reason is ineffective by itself. Belief without emotion of any kind has no effect on the will. It is only because we care about the outcome that we act. Here was the overturning of emphasis that Baier found so compelling. It is not Hume, the Sophist, who is her collaborator, but Hume who left in ruins a tripartite model of the soul that dates back to Plato. The ideal of a controlling reason, ruling over spirit and emotion, credited with much of the superiority of "Western" man, is demolished. "Reason is, and ought only to be the slave of the passions, and can never pretend to any other office than to serve and obey them" (Treatise, II, III, Section ii, p. 415). The moral at the end of Book I of the Treatise, said Baier, is not that there is no truth, but that reason cut off from emotion, from civility, and from the normal impulses of sympathy and self-interest, must destroy itself. Reason is nothing without the direction of passion. Reason cut off from concern and debate is monstrous, but Hume's final conclusion is not skeptical. It is reconstructive. Reading on to Books II and III, says Baier, it becomes clear that the moral of the Treatise is not that reason should be abandoned but that it should be "enlarged" to include response to others, caring judgment, and shared moral sentiment, the very elements promoted in feminist philosophy.

Baier did not coolly and analytically dissect and critique arguments. Traditionally adversarial, philosophers have for the most part read past philosophers as either right or wrong. A properly philosophical reading isolates positions and analyzes arguments as valid or invalid. Alternatively, competitive interpretation can take center stage, and a scholar can make a name for herself by proposing and defending novel or contentious interpretations of texts. Baier's meditation on Hume in Progress of Sentiments proceeded on different principles. The point was neither to criticize nor to come up with what Hume "really" meant or said. Places where Hume is not clear or consistent were taken for granted as part of Hume's thinking. The point was not to prove Hume right or wrong, but to attempt to think along with him through the crucial bottlenecks where thoughts become tangled and inconsistent. On this approach, a work of philosophy like the Treatise is not a series of timeless logical or illogical steps, but a train of thought in narrative sequence that Baier as contemporary philosopher retraces and extends. Instead of stopping at the astonishing proposition that the idea of enduring substances or minds is a fiction, Baier followed Hume on to the next idea, in which these fictions are ways, perhaps even necessary ways, to organize experience. In the famous skeptical conclusion to Book I, Hume is in despair, lost at sea; he can find no foothold for belief. Are we to take his despair seriously? Are we to hear a mocking parody of Descartes's despair in the *Meditations*? Baier listens attentively to separate out irony from assertion. She waits to hear what aspects of Hume's skepticism will be abandoned as he moves on into the more constructive Books II and III.

Baier's sympathetic and participatory reading of Hume required not just analysis of assertion and argument, but an ear for style and tone. It required not just logical acumen, but a feeling for Hume the man. She did not claim for such a reading that it is the only correct reading. Others may hear what Hume says differently, just as in conversation what is said can be understood differently by different participants. The model, Baier said, was Hume's own. Philosophy in Hume's enlarged sense is a cooperative endeavor, not conducted in solitude or barricaded with argument against response, but open to communication and response.

But is it safe to follow along so trustingly the thought of another philosopher, to put so much into understanding and so little into suspicion? What kind of knowledge is this social and sentimental knowledge that is to give added support to a reconstructed feminist epistemology? Does it doom feminist proposals to relative truth? Does it mean that feminists have no decisive weapons with which to defeat claims that women are inferior? Does it remove women from participating fully in philosophy as it is currently practiced in prestigious academic institutions? Will it disqualify feminist essays for publication in leading philosophy journals? Will it, just as Hume feared for himself, expose feminists to "the enmity of all metaphysicians, logicians, mathematicians, and even theologians" (*Treatise*, I, IV, Section vii, p. 264)? What kind of mind is claimed by Hume and Baier as the human mind? A feminine mind? An inferior mind? Without authority? Doomed to passive reaction? To following along with custom? Following socialized instincts? Could not this be seen as reversion to feminine stereotypes and feminine powerlessness? Even more important, what has happened to critical reflection, which seems to require an adversarial stance against others as well as against one's own vested ideas?

Baier's Hume is no nihilist. He does not reject all critical reflection and reason. After the skeptical arguments, Baier argued, he reconstructed a more "careless" or "carefree" reasonableness, a reasonableness that is protective against error and that allows non-dogmatic assertions of truth. First, Hume recognized a natural animal instinct of good sense. Although in non-human forms good sense operates in a narrow prescribed sphere, the sheer number of ideas that humans generate in their hyperactive imagination and memory adds a further dimension. Given the fecundity of their ideas, said Hume, humans are pressed to choose, pressed to highlight ideas with the most force and vivacity, and pressed to suppress others as less important. Still there is nothing in this extension of animal "good sense" to mental housekeeping that has normative force. From the standpoint of critical reflection, the most forceful and vivid of our ideas could turn out to be wrong. Certainly ideas of women expressed by Hume and other modern philosophers were nothing if not vivid.

But Baier and other defenders of Hume were able to point to passages in which Hume seems to allow for further correction of error. For example in Book III of the *Treatise* Hume admits that adjustment of sentiment-based judgments is necessary. Hume's ethics are based on natural sympathy, a sympathy felt most acutely for those nearest to us, and most acutely of all for ourselves. Sympathy for others, especially if they are not family and friends, will almost always, says Hume, be overruled by strong self-interest. But, said Hume, it is also "natural" for people to correct their partial moral judgments, by "calm determinations of the passions founded on some distant view or reflection" (*Treatise*, III, III, Section i, pp. 582–3). The reason Hume gives is pragmatic. If a man judges solely on the basis of his own interests, difficulties arise. First, given that his interests will inevitably conflict with other men's interests, he will find himself constantly contradicted in conversation. Secondly, he will not be able to maintain consistency of judgment as his own interests change. One year with a high income he will be against taxes; the next year being unemployed he will want more progressive rates. Given the discomfort of both controversy and inconsistency, says Hume, a man is forced to seek some more general, more philosophic, standard of judgment based on a wider sympathy with others. Such a sentiment does not come near to being as lively as self-interest, or interest in family and friends. It does not arouse strong passions of love and hate and can easily be overcome by those passions. But given its greater steadiness and its calming effect, it is at least sometimes able to subdue the more heated emotions (*Treatise*, III, III, Section i, pp. 582–4).

Even here feminists might have qualms. Will such a reflective reason be of use in correcting racist or misogynous misconceptions? An Englishman, with interests abroad, may naturally have trouble being sympathetic with

Indians, Africans, or Muslims who seem to interfere with profitable trade. Closer to home, a man with everything to gain from a wife who devotes herself to his needs may have trouble being sympathetic with a woman's unhappiness in her restricted life. But it is hard to see how such partiality is likely to be corrected in the process described by Hume. At his club, and at fashionable dinners, such a man consorts with men whose interests coincide with his own. Certainly he is unlikely to find himself in conversation with Indians, Muslims, or Africans. He speaks with his wife, but she is a lone voice and his self-interest in domestic matters is so well settled and institutionally established that it is hard to see why he should suffer the variability in interest that would cause him the embarrassment of inconsistency. Small disagreements among communities of broadly common interest can be adjusted in this way, but not the overturning of institutionalized prejudice shared by men who socialize with their own class and gender. Baier comments on Hume's insistence in his *History of England* and essays on government on the importance of established venues for political discussion, but there is no reason to think that women, foreigners, or working-class English men would have any standing in those venues.

Should not a feminist expect more from philosophy? Baier found in Hume a powerful ally against philosophic presumption, and a corrective to certain kinds of feminist extremism. An "unreflective" feminist might reject reason out of hand as identified with masculine privilege, a position hard to maintain without absurdity. She might learn from Hume, as Baier suggests, a more subtle approach. The problem with the philosopher's solitary intellectualist reason is not only that philosophic reason has been in complicity with conservative politics; Hume's more deflating observation is reason's and academic philosophy's powerlessness. Speculative reason cannot, in fact, command belief. No matter how many clever arguments establish that the external world is an illusion or that the future might not be like the past, we continue to believe by habit and instinct. Reason without the imagination and sentiment that establishes belief is a dead letter. It does not command belief; it does not provide a motive for any kind of action. It is moribund, an academic specialty with no impact on beliefs or actions.

Why, asks Hume at the end of Book II, do philosophers philosophize? What is the sentiment that drives them when there is no apparent utility in philosophy for themselves or others? Is it simply love of the game of reasoning, pleasure in finding a solution to a puzzle-problem? But even in hunting or gaming, there has to be a quarry, a goal with at least pretended importance.

Philosophers do regularly include a paragraph or two at the beginning or end of their treatises explaining the importance of what they are about to prove or have already proven. But do philosophers care about that goal any more than a hunter cares about the few partridges that he shoots? Philosophers, said Hume, can take a kind of distant abstract interest in the academic possibility of a result, just as a military expert surveying the fortifications of a foreign enemy city might idly estimate the fortifications' efficiency without any real interest in the defense of that city, but it is hard to think that this is what drives philosophers to page after page of the dense reasoning typical in philosophical writing.

Hume was candid about the reasons for his own return to philosophy after the skeptical doubts of Book I. In so far as philosophy takes as its goal the factual understanding of human nature, he was curious. How do the mechanisms of the mind work? What is the cause of various passions? How are governments structured? There is pleasure in finding some principle behind phenomena so as to guard against surprise and false expectations. And, perhaps even more important, he was ambitious, a motive freely admitted by the disarming Hume. He wanted very much to make a name for himself, which he was successful in doing after he turned away from abstruse reasoning to a more popular style of writing in his *Essays*. There is, he pointed out, a further benefit of "careless" philosophizing: it keeps the mind occupied and off more dangerous speculation in religion. "Superstition" disturbs people in their life and actions; philosophy, calmer and less agitated, incites no one to action. If a man is able to give up both philosophy and religion and live without too many questions that is best. The practical man, said Hume, should not be disturbed (*Treatise*, II, III, Section x, pp. 448–54). If a man, a man like himself, however, has an active mind and is not content with a merely practical life, philosophy is preferred to religion as the lesser of evils.

The question, of course, is not whether feminists might be tempted to question the adequacy for feminist purposes of Hume's calm, distant, harmless philosophic curiosity, but whether in wanting more they are not guilty of the excessive zeal condemned as dangerous by Hume and Baier. Baier herself took no radical feminist stances; she did not call for an end to heterosexuality, demand paychecks for homemakers, or a boycott of mothering. But it is hard to see how even moderate feminist reforms can be strongly defended given Hume's "careless" "love of truth."

Following Hume's lead, a feminist might defend probable reasoning from cause and effect following rules of practice laid down by Hume (*Treatise*, I,

III, Section xv, p. 173). She might defend a natural process of corrective "reflection," in which the ruling passion of self-interest is tempered by second thoughts that tell us that "the passion [of greed] is much better satisfied by its restraint, than by its liberty." She might tell those with radical sentiments "that by preserving society, we make much greater advances in the acquiring of possessions, than by running into the solitary and forlorn condition, which must follow upon violence and universal license" (Treatise, III, II, Section ii, p. 492). She might approve the study of history and different forms of government to help sort out the general usefulness of various institutions. She might praise with Hume practical "intellectual virtues," virtues that help a man or woman to succeed in the world and make him or her a good partner in business, virtues such as "industry, perseverance, patience, activity, application, constancy" (Treatise, III, III, Section iv, p. 610). She could adopt a style of reasoning that is "carefree," witty, and open, not barricaded behind absolute truth, claiming only probability. She could acknowledge that beliefs and judgments are based on no necessarily true foundations, and must always be submitted to others for their understanding and confirmation. The question remains: is this enough for feminist purposes? Is it enough to force the changes that feminists demand?

Further readings

Various feminist appropriations and criticisms of Hume can be found in Bat-Ami Bar On's edited collection, Modern Engendering: Critical Feminist Readings in Modern Western Philosophy, and in Anne Jacobson's collection, Feminist Interpretations of David Hume. Genevieve Lloyd's essay "Hume and the Passion for Truth" in the Jacobson collection to some degree endorses Baier's Humean alternative to rationalism, but also finds other integrative alternatives to rationalism in the early modern period and argues that they are not original with Hume. Annette Baier's books, all of which deal in one way or another with Humean perspectives, include, in addition to A Progress of Sentiments, The Commons of the Mind in which she extends Humean attitudes to several areas of philosophy, and Postures of the Mind: Essays on Mind and Morals, a collection of her early essays focusing on Hume's critique of rationalism and its applications to ethics.

7

FEMINIST ANTINOMIES
Immanuel Kant

If Hume has been hailed as a friend of feminists, Kant has often been declared the enemy. Feminists have rejected his rationalist ethics as the antithesis of feminine caring. They have charged his "unity of apperception" with being a prototype for illegitimate masculine authority and Western hubris. They have condemned "pure" reason as the sovereignty of "rational man" over feminine connectiveness. Where Hume emphasized the sociability of custom and habit, Kant idealized a delusive individualism that severs human ties. Where Hume approved feeling as the basis of morality, Kant made emotion the downfall of virtue.

In *Cognition and Eros*, Robin Schott traced a history from Plato to Kant of the idea that understanding and feeling are in opposition and that women, identified with eros, are a threat to knowledge. Such views, she charged, are typical of philosophy. They support and further male dominance. She described her own difficulty in accepting this judgment. Brought up in an analytic tradition with roots in seventeenth- and eighteenth-century rationalism, "schooled in the philosophical tradition of objectivity," it was hard for her to conclude that universal forms of knowledge were not needed. At the same time, as a woman, she felt alienated, not capable of the detachment from feeling and relation that Kantian reason seemed to require. She had to "dirty" her hands in social history, she said, before she could free herself from the illusion of rational autonomy imposed on her by philosophical training. She had to go back in history for "original ascetic impulses" that distanced reason from physical desire. She had to combine these with a modern "flight from the body" blamed on "commodity capitalism" (*Cognition and Eros*, pp. ix–x). Philosophy, Schott concluded, is not "pure" reason. It has historical content. Seemingly neutral metaphysics and epistemology reflect and support oppressive social relations. Philosophy in its Kantian and neo-Kantian forms promotes capitalist alienation and validates women's exclusion from higher education, politics, and the work force.

Other feminists were in agreement, citing Kant as a primary example of alienated masculinity and fraudulent universality. Kristen Waters, in "Women in Kantian Ethics" (in Bar On (ed.), *Modern Engendering*), found a failure of universality both in Kant's early precritical aesthetics where women are treated as objects rather than as human ends and in his late *Anthropology* where women's potential is limited to their role in reproduction. Problems with gender, said Jean Rumsey, infect Kant's moral agency ("Revisions of Agency in Kant's Moral Theory" in Schott (ed.), *Feminist Interpretations of Immanuel Kant*). Instead of a balanced view of human action, he takes his idea of agency from a narrow group of men of his own time, class, and nationality, men who are self-willed and grasping, with a drive to independence and mastery and a fear of affiliation and intimacy.

But feminist critics could also show considerable ambivalence when contemplating a wholesale rejection of Kantian themes. Other essays in the Bar On and Schott collections gave Kant mixed reviews. Adrian Piper ("Xenophobia and Kantian Rationalism" in *Feminist Interpretations*) argued that if feminists adopted Strawson's narrow interpretation of Kant's transcendental necessity, Kant's unity of apperception could help to explain racism and show how an expanded conception of "man" might be synthesized from wider experience. Holly Wilson, "Rethinking Kant from the Perspective of Ecofeminism," found something to admire in the third critique's recognition of vitality and purpose (in Schott (ed.), *Feminist Interpretations*). Also in Schott's collection, Marcia Moen found "Feminist Themes in Unlikely Places," namely in Kant's *Critique of Judgment*. Although Kant was too much committed to the "atomic individual" fully to conceptualize a feminine "relational self," his last critique, she said, linked knowing with feeling and acting. As a consequence, he was able to make steps in a feminist direction. Although he was "blocked" by limits inherent in the oppositional categories he inherited from philosophical tradition, he provided glimpses of a new kind of "cultural participant" as alternative to an autonomous rational knower. Especially promising if not decisive, said Moen, was Kant's reference to the "communicability" of aesthetic pleasure.

Some who explicitly compared Hume and Kant did not single-mindedly award the feminist laurel to Hume. Marcia Brown ("Kantian Ethics and Claims of Detachment" in *Feminist Interpretations*) argued that although Kant was hampered by his masculinity and downgraded emotion as a component in morality, his emphasis on detachment and universality might in the end be more conducive to social change than the socially conservative custom and habit highlighted by Hume. Nancy Tuana in *Woman and the History of Philosophy* was critical of Kant, but found Hume not much better. As she put it, her "initial prediction that women would fare better with a moral theory like that of Hume, which incorporates emotion, than with one like Kant's, which excludes emotion from moral obligation, was erroneous. Despite significant differences in moral theory, Kant and Hume hold surprisingly similar positions concerning woman's moral capabilities" (*Woman and the History of Philosophy*, p. 81). The difference as far as women are concerned, said Tuana, is one of degree: Kant holds that women are incapable of moral agency, Hume that they are less capable.

Tuana in her introduction laid out some of the maxims that should guide feminist judgments of this sort. A feminist philosopher, she said, should read philosophy "like a woman." She should be conscious of her sex. She should focus on views expressed about her sex. She should be aware of the gender identity of the philosopher she reads and how gender affects his views. She should be ready to suggest alternate perspectives that come out of women's experiences. Guided by such maxims, said Tuana, a woman reader of philosophy can critically assess approaches to ethics by asking: Does the philosopher in question describe women as possible moral agents? Does he value traits traditionally associated with masculinity? Does he see women as different morally? Does he describe morality as control of or exclusion of traits traditionally associated with femininity? By those standards, said Tuana, neither Kant nor Hume can be approved.

Tuana's "reading like a woman" was, of course, heterodox in analytic circles where material relating to social prejudice or politics is typically edited out as irrelevant. A philosophical reading is supposed to be an intellectual reading, a reading of the mind that has nothing to do with the sex of a reader anymore than it has to do with any fact about bodies or physical circumstance. Nor, on this view, should philosophical critique be based on social utility. Philosophical approval should depend on clarity of definition, validity of argument, and consistency of principles, not on whether a theory advances the interests of the reader or of any social group to which she or he belongs. As noted by Schott, this ideal of objective dispassionate critique has a long pedigree going back to Descartes and Kant, and before them to Plato and Aristotle. It shaped twentieth-century movements of positivism and linguistic analysis. It continues to influence contemporary logical semantics and naturalized epistemology.

To many philosophers working within the profession it makes no sense to speak as Tuana did of experience as sexed or of gender generating different readings or evaluations of epistemology or metaphysics. Sense data are experienced by men and women. Men and women speak a common language. Logic is the same for men and women. A focus on women's issues or any other social issues when reading philosophy is to rob philosophy of its last remaining authority and turn it to special pleading with no claim to truth and no academic standing. The dispute was not only between feminists and non-feminist philosophers, but also between feminists. Should a woman entering a field like philosophy, traditionally dominated by men, "read as a woman," that is as an alienated outsider to tradition. Or should she read "like a man," that is read attempting faithfully to honor methods and maxims that currently govern the discipline of philosophy. For many women philosophers, reading like a woman was an admission of failure to meet professional standards.

The dispute was occurring not only in philosophy but also in other areas of knowledge. Feminists lined up on either side of the question of whether knowledge is always relative and from a limited perspective, or whether with the proper methods universal truths can be discovered. Some adopted a "standpoint" view of knowledge, arguing that existing philosophy or existing science is from the point of view of the dominant social group, white Western men. This, in turn, could be used to explain why women and men of disadvantaged groups are underrepresented in science or philosophy even when legal barriers to their participation have been removed. Further supporting the standpoint view were mainstream lines of twentieth-century theory that relativized knowledge. The popular changing paradigm view of Thomas Kuhn made the epistemological standards of one scientific era incommensurable with those of other eras. "Science studies" in the 1980s and 1990s documented social factors shaping scientific problems and research methods. Marx's critique of "bourgeois" science as ideological made forms of knowledge depend on economic interests. If, as Marx demanded, science in Western countries should be a worker's science, geared to workers' needs and activities, it was only a small step to a further demand. Science should be from the standpoint of progressive workers, and also from the standpoint of the subjugated sex-class of women.

Feminist studies proliferated, exploring "women's ways of knowing" based on traditional women's work like mothering, social work, or nursing. Historians Susan Bordo and Carolyn Merchant searched back in history for premodern perspectives of knowledge more consistent with a "woman's" standpoint, models in which the relation between man/woman and nature was no longer one of domination but one of respect and interaction, or in which intuition and sympathy generate knowledge rather than logic and manipulative experiment.

But in the rush to standpoint theory there was much second thought, and for those feminist critics who remained more orthodox in their approach to knowledge, even outrage. Standpoint theory was untenable, they argued. It threatened to leave women behind in the great advance of modern enlightenment that had brought the West to its present advanced state of scientific and political development. It devalued the relative emancipation of women in Western countries, an emancipation based on women's rational abilities. Science is needed to establish the fact that common views concerning women's incapacity are false. Philosophy is needed to prove that there is no rationally consistent way to exclude women from political participation. By not availing themselves of reason, feminists defeated their cause. If truth is always a matter of perspective or socially determined cognitive paradigms, how can feminist critique prevail or feminist truth be established? Feminist truth might be tolerated along with other free expression, but feminists would lack the authority to force change. Standpoint theorists might theorize about inclusion and diversity, but women and men of color would continue to be discouraged from entering masculine fields, and would be until they are able to make the claim that their methods are superior and their conclusions true. Women researchers might found alternative establishments in which to do science "as women"; they might try to win some acceptance for values "traditionally identified as feminine"; they could try to eliminate methods or policies that excluded or undervalued those qualities. Their efforts would remain marginal and underfunded.

Two equally unacceptable and mutually contradictory alternatives both seemed unavoidable. On one hand, all knowledge must be from a particular standpoint—women's, European, men's, third world, African-American. All knowledge must begin from necessarily different experiences and be constructed according to linguistic and discursive regularities that are culturally variable. If this is the case, truth, except in a very limited and relative sense, is an illusion and power politics must decide which of competing views prevails. At the same time, there are matters of fact, and the possibility must exist of an accurate representation of those facts. A sure foundation and a universally effective method can and must be found that leads to the discovery and communication of truths common to all. Women experience and understand the world in ways that are different from ways in which men experience and understand the world, but if there is no common standard of truth, feminist claims have no authority outside feminist circles.

Whatever complaints feminists might have about Kant's views on women, this modernist "antinomy" is at the heart of Kantian metaphysics. Surveying two centuries of political and intellectual turmoil, Kant worked his way through the major philosophers of the modern period. He was a rationalist with Wolff, then "roused from dogmatic slumber" by Hume's skeptical arguments. He rejected religious enthusiasm with Locke and thrilled to Rousseau's stirring calls for freedom and nature. He rejected the genre rules of classical aesthetics and turned instead to Baumgarten's felt sensibility to natural beauty. But out of those intellectual movements, he believed, had come no clear modern vision of the world, and no hope that with more thought one was forthcoming. Modern thought had stalled, mired down in incoherence. No matter how many new observations were made in astronomy, cosmology could make no coherent sense of time and space. Physics assumed and did not assume that matter is infinitely divisible. There was no room for God in the scientific view of the world, but some first cause is necessary. Scientists must think that every event is determined by prior causes, but must also acknowledge that intentional action requires that some events be uncaused.

Kantian epistemology is generated out of antinomy. Cartesian science projected an authoritative method of inquiry based on innate and necessarily true rational principles universally valid for all researchers. But once the proofs for the existence of God that Descartes used to support the veracity of innate ideas were abandoned, Humean skepticism seemed inevitable. None of a person's ideas, whether its origin is inside the mind or outside the mind, can be counted on to represent objective reality. All a would-be knower has is his or her own experience, private and personal ideas that vary according to situation and predilection. Although Locke retained much of Cartesianism, including the assumption that rational principles govern the sorting and abstracting of ideas, by Hume all last remaining universality due to reason was compromised. Only shifting personal phenomenal flux of perception is left, along with unvalidated, customary, habitual, and instinctual ways of combining and imaginatively augmenting perception. Here as understood by Kant was the modern dilemma. All knowledge must be from variable human experience; at the same time, some sort of knowledge must be possible.

On the one hand, it appears that all experience is personal, conditioned by an individual's particular place in space and time and in no way universal. Nor does it seem that there is any method or insight that can transcend that perspective to produce knowledge not mediated by an individual man's or woman's experience. Given that all experience is phenomenal, the only possible true judgment is the judgment that something appears a certain way to me, and even this minimal judgment, once a general word is used to characterize the experience, is questionable. Is a certain kind of behavior "sexual harassment"? A woman experiences it as such, but the man who initiates the behavior sees it as flattery or courtship. A simple claim to be experiencing "something or other" makes no claim to truth or universality; as a result feminist complaints have no more authority that those of any other group.

On the other hand, the force of the language used to make knowledge claims implies something very different. To say that a certain kind of behavior is harassing is not to express feelings but to characterize that behavior. To say, as the microbiologist and feminist historian of science Evelyn Fox Keller said, that the supposition of a pacemaker cell cannot account for slime mold aggregation is not to propose an alternative "woman's" feeling for organic processes. It is to say that the thesis that all cellular processes can be explained by linear causal mechanisms is false ("The Force of the Pacemaker Concept in Theories of Aggregation in Cellular Slime Mold" in Reflections on Gender and Science, pp. 150–7). Similarly geneticist Barbara McClintock's claim that transposition of genes occurs in multicelled organisms asserts that the opposing theory of genes as atomistic determinants is false and misleads research. The difference is described by Keller, ruminating on the importance of McClintock's work. It is not that McClintock worked from a "feminist consciousness, or even from a female consciousness," said Keller. Instead her revolutionary work came out of the "determination to claim science as a human rather than a male endeavor" (Reflections, p. 175). Being a woman and to some degree an outsider may have allowed McClintock to see more clearly false assumptions that distort reality, but her claim to truth is no less universal. The huge resources and energy devoted to science only make sense on the assumption that, regardless of appearances, there is an underlying reality, including the process of genetic inheritance, a reality potentially intelligible to the human mind.

The feminist dilemma between standpoint and empiricist epistemologies leads to a further ontological antinomy also with Kantian roots. A critical reading of philosophy in Tuana's sense of "reading like a woman" requires identification of "feminine" and "masculine" characteristics. The feminist critic looks for evidence that traits associated with femininity are devalued. She looks for evidence that traits associated with masculinity have been made the basis for virtue. She searches for alternate feminine ways to think about morality. "Femininity" is an essential cluster of characteristics in contrast to "masculinity" with its own defining features. Again an antinomy of two contradictory but seemingly true principles emerges. On the one hand femininity and masculinity are matters of fact, and terms naming those facts figure prominently in feminist critique. The distinguishing features of men and women must be identified if manifestations of the power imbalance between them are to be brought to light. If masculinity and femininity are indiscernible, dominance relations between women and men will be indiscernible, submerged in empty counter-factual assumptions of human uniformity. To see how gender affects philosophy or any field of knowledge, it is necessary to define what gender is, to establish the categories that are the basis for feminist judgments of gender inequity or bias.

On the other hand, it seems also inescapably true that "femininity" and "masculinity" are not things-in-themselves, not objective fact, and name no prelinguistic essence. Instead they are nominal essences, variable social constructs without universal applicability. On this view femininity and masculinity mark a shifting bias that, far from being bedrock for feminist analysis, should be jettisoned as theoretically and practically suspect. To look for the feminine, worse to valorize the feminine, is to return women to social stereotypes that constrain their behavior.

Here again "antinomy" generated passionate and heated discussion among feminists, this time centered on "essentialism." In the 1980s, social psychologist Carol Gilligan's claim that women had a different "moral voice" challenged feminist philosophers to develop alternative feminist ethics. Care and relation were made the basis of moral responsibility to supplement or replace Kantian rationalist ethics based on justice or universal principle. Also again there was heated opposition. Should any voice or moral style be identified as "feminine"? Does a "feminine" virtue of care reimprison women in the straitjacket of a false universal, relegating them once again to service work and self-sacrificial nurturance with feminist sanction. Or does such a perspective return women to a true and previously devalued feminine essence? Both theses seem true; both seem impossible. On the one hand femininity must be defined and defended if feminism is to have content. On the other hand, any such identification threatens to "imprison" women in the strait-jacket of essence and restrict their "perfectibility".

This antinomy also can be traced back to modernist debates as understood and confronted by Kant. On the one hand, the prevailing Christianized Aristotelianism of the medieval schools took for granted the existence of form in nature. If nature is formless, it is uncategorizable and therefore unknowable. The types of living organisms in general and the form of man in particular are obvious prototypes. Man, like other substances, has an ideal essence or nature, characterized by rationality, autonomy, and free will, an essence that defines him as a specific species of being. In turn, the form of man allows for sub-essences like masculinity and femininity, variants due to degeneration, changed circumstance, or specific function. Particular races may be designed as natural slaves, lower classes as less rational, women as a subspecies designed for specialized biological functions. On the other hand, from the perspective of the new experimental and mechanical sciences there are no fixed forms in nature, only changing and shifting patterns of obser-vation that humans sort, abstract from, and causally relate in a variety of ways in order to isolate probable mechanisms that can be plotted and predicted.

The word "man," Locke said, denotes a nominal, not a real essence. It is an abstraction of the human mind from necessarily limited experience. On this view there is no essential masculinity or femininity in nature, only a vari-ety of appearances which, given similarities and differences, can be put into provisional categories. Hume went a step further. There is no reason why appearances might not change, no reason why apparent similarities might fail, no reason why women might not suddenly take on masculine character-istics or men's lifestyles, or men suddenly become feminine. No reason why a man might not become a woman or a woman a man. No reason why a gorilla might not give birth to a man. Or a man to a gorilla. To think that this could not or would necessarily not happen is a matter of custom and habit, not reason.

Again there are consequences for feminist theory. If there is such a thing as femininity it is women who are its exemplars, and the defense and advancement of women must involve the discovery, defense, and promotion of femininity and consequently of women's ways of knowing and feminine voices in philosophy. If on the other hand femininity is a nominal essence, either an artifact of sexist discourse or due to habit or custom that relegates women to nurturance or emotionality, then femininity must be denounced, resisted, and, in the end, eradicated. The current idea of femininity might be as misguided as Locke's little white boy's idea that light skin is a defining characteristic of humanity. In that case, to read as a woman looking for feminine characteristics might support and maintain the construction of inferiorized gender identity. But the nominalist position also has pitfalls. What is to be the basis for feminist critique or feminist philosophy? If there is no femininity, or even, as some radical theorists argued, no "women," if there is no "masculine" dominance as guideline, from what perspective or evaluative stance can a woman approach philosophy or any other tradition? If she has no grounded feminine essence, what is to be her feminist goal or purpose?

Kant took a keen interest in the question of essence. He was both aware of and fascinated by natural history. He read Buffon. He knew the taxonomic innovations of Linnaeus. Early in his career he debated with Georg Forster, artist/scientist with the Cook expedition, about human origins. Africans and Caribbeans may look and act differently from Europeans, but science is not and cannot be only a collation of constant conjunctions, said Kant. Science has to orient itself by certain principles, one of which is that there is some purpose in nature beyond the random proliferation of unrelated organic mechanisms. Given the principle of teleology in nature, he concluded, one can see that what accounts for human diversity is not separate origins but the fact that humans are "designed" for maximum adaptability in a wide range of environments ("On the Use of Teleological Principles in Nature," Part II of Critique of Judgment). Modern science brought to light the great and seemingly meaningless, purposeless, and disordered diversity and complexity of living organisms discovered macroscopically in exploration and microscopically with the tools of modern optics. But it could not, it seemed to Kant, eliminate the practical and theoretical necessity for form and function, for femininity, masculinity, for different species of animal, for categorizable human variation. Kant would devote the second half of the Critique of Judgment to understanding this conflict. The goal of modern science, he agreed, must be to find mechanical explanations for all phenomena without recourse to form or function. On the other hand, biological research would chase chimeras, if it did not take as presupposition an intuitive sense of functional purpose.

If the first part of Kant's third Critique on aesthetic judgment gets little attention from contemporary philosophers, they have been even less interested in Kant's speculations on form and purpose in nature. Given the prevailing view that chance mechanisms of mutation and natural selection govern organic change and the perceived danger that any mention of design in nature gives credence to science's old enemy theology, it can seem irrational even to entertain the idea of purpose in nature. But, said Kant, in actual scientific practice, especially in biology, purpose is a necessary operating assumption. A biologist needs the "guiding thread" of organic function if she is not to collate meaningless data.

Keller traces the continuing twentieth-century history of Kant's antinomy in *Refiguring Life*. The dominant strand in modern biology continued to focus on mechanism, this time genetic mechanism. All illicit reference to "teleology"—to form, function, or purpose—was eliminated. The goal of science was to find linear causal mechanisms that can be duplicated in the laboratory or clinic and used for genetically engineered crops, genetic therapies, and in vitro reproductive techniques. Researchers in microbiology searched for formulas that account for the ways a gene produces a biological effect by way of a chain of duplicable reactions. As research continued, however, it became clear through the work of McClintock and others, argued Keller, that such an approach cannot do justice to organic processes that are often or even always interactive and self-organizing. McClintock made her discoveries by thinking not in terms of chains of impacting molecules, but in terms of purpose. When she noted patterns in coloration in corn, an intuition of adaptive purpose led her to the interactive processes by which genetic changes were carried out, processes that had been ruled out by current assumptions of genetic determinism. In fact, self-regulating organic processes could not be understood only in terms of linear causality. The standard empiricist model of objective observation and logical deduction had been valuable but was insufficient for understanding.

McClintock's subject was corn. When applied to human organisms, the question of form and purpose is even more difficult. What is the purpose of a man? Or a woman? Proud, independent, social, caring, heterosexual, self-interested? Even if it is taken for granted that all characteristics evolve by chance mutation and natural selection, in providing the evidence and illustration that even evolution requires, antinomy resurfaces. How is a biologist to make sense of organic form sufficiently so as to trace an evolutionary progression? What is to count as an individual trait? Are feminine and masculine traits to be automatically approved as validated in natural selection? Or is there a human function and form that can be altered or distorted by chance mutation or environmental stress. Which traits are to be altered or removed by education, upbringing, or medical intervention? These questions, given the development of new forms of genetic selection and therapy, are no longer only theoretical.

The problem of form in nature can be taken to a further level of antinomy, again with Kantian roots. Given a mechanistic view of natural processes, how are feminist purposes or any human purposes to be understood? Contemporary genetic research deepens the antinomy as more and more human traits, including masculinity and femininity, are linked to specific genetic variations, and techniques of genetic manipulation are developed. Genetic explanations both support mechanism as the reality behind all appearance and allow for change subject to human desire. Are human purposes equally and blindly determined by genes or are they freely chosen and undetermined? Given new genetic interventions, women can be made more or less "feminine." Homosexuals can be "treated" by genetic therapies to be more or less heterosexual. Masculine characteristics can be enhanced to make better warriors or athletes. Racial characteristics might be altered or suppressed. On the one hand the goal of science must and should be the utmost reach of mechanical molecular explanation, with the assumption that all physical phenomena are caused by chains of impacting atoms. On the other hand, the fact that humans engage in freely chosen action and judge actions good or bad assumes that not all phenomena are caused, that some choices are available, and that some interventions may not be consistent with human purpose or form. Keller quotes the founder of quantum theory, Erwin Schroedinger.

> Let's see whether we cannot draw the correct, noncontradictory conclusion from the following two premises:
> My body functions as a pure mechanism according to the Laws of Nature.
> Yet I know, by incontrovertible direct experience, that I am directing its motions.
>
> (Refiguring Life, p. 77)

Feminists are in no position to give up either of Schroedinger's premises. Any progressive movement must document oppression, trace its causes and its necessary effects on victims, find out the mechanisms that lead to its perpetuation. On the other hand every progressive movement must also hold out hope for change. Feminist research in history and social science painstakingly documents male dominance and traces its varied causes and effects. Feminist philosophers expose the social inequalities that generate discriminatory theories of rights or justice. Scientists like Keller and McClintock explore the complicated process of genetic inheritance. Kant's synthetic a priori principle of human cognition that every event has a cause drives on these inquiries. It cannot just have happened without cause that in so many cultures and eras women have had less power than men and their lack of power persists. The great success of feminist social science is to have shown the deep social and psychological determinants of sexual inequality and the economic, psychic, and even biological mechanisms that hold it in place. The great success of feminist philosophy is to show how inequality is embedded in the very ideas with which we think. As Kant put one side of the antinomy: "There is no freedom; everything in the world takes place solely in accordance with laws of nature" (*Critique of Pure Reason*, p. 409).

But this thesis, seemingly the foundation for modern science, is fatal for moral or progressive action, including feminist action. If a moral agent or political activist not only envisions change but hopes to be effective in promoting change, she must, it seems, be able to interrupt causal sequences. If not, a feminist might dream of communities of women scholars or laboratories in which diverse methods are respected, but she could not hope for them. Given the necessary causal determinants of material life there is no reason to think that such projects could be realized as a result of her intentions. For feminist projects to be effective, for there to be any hope that feminists might change the world for the better, the anti-thesis is necessary. Again as stated by Kant: "Causality in accordance with laws of nature is not the only causality from which the appearances of the world can one and all be derived. To explain these appearances it is necessary to assume that there is also another causality, that of freedom" (*Critique of Pure Reason*, p. 409).

As in other Kantian antinomies, strong and apparently irrefutable arguments show the unacceptability and impossibility of both alternatives—of causal determinacy and of free will. If spontaneous uncaused beginnings are allowed, the unity of nature and therefore the basis for science is undermined. An uncaused cause "is not to be met with in any experience, and is therefore an empty thought-entity" (*Critique of Pure Reason*, p. 410). On the other hand, the universality of causation is incoherent not only in that it rules out free action but also in that it assumes an endless regress of causes with no beginning at all.

Standpoint as opposed to empiricist epistemologies, essentialist as opposed to nominal ontologies, mechanistic determinism as opposed to free will: might a postmodern feminist simply lay these metaphysical antinomies aside? Should she follow the lead of contemporary pragmatists like Richard Rorty and reduce antinomy to a conversation topic without pressing existential significance? Should she stop worrying the issue of standpoint as opposed to empiricist approaches to knowledge and adopt a naturalized epistemology? Should she accept science as an extension of animal survival tactics and applaud its "success" in promoting physical survival and the maximization of "pleasurable stimulations"? Should she become a scientific realist, avoiding antinomy in the opposite direction by allowing science to have the last word on the nature of "things-in-themselves"?

For feminists concerned about the misrepresentation of women in science or philosophy, or with establishing a common cause between women of diverse races, or developing realistic goals and purposes for feminist politics, a relaxed and accepting antimetaphysical attitude is difficult to sustain. For women conscious of bias in science and the historic exclusion of work by women that does not fit established paradigms, objectivity cannot be guaranteed simply by accepting science's choice of objects and methods. How is the supposed "success" of science to be measured? In terms of weapons systems? Or the elimination of trouble-making behavior? Which pleasurable stimulations are to be maximized? Pornographic stimulations? Violent video games? Faced with these questions, good-natured acceptance of a variety of metaphysical and epistemological views as part of philosophical "conversation" is hard to maintain.

In Critique of Pure Reason Kant proposed three questions that metaphysics must try to answer. What can I know? What should I do? What can I hope for? These metaphysical questions might well be asked by a feminist reading philosophy.

First. What can I know? Does a philosopher's theory of knowledge preclude feminist agency? Does the philosopher indicate what methods and procedures in science and in the philosophic oversight of science will be most conducive to the production of knowledge useful in furthering progressive goals. Does the philosopher indicate what kind of scientific community can best deliver that knowledge?

Second: What should I do? Is there an account of moral agency given by the philosopher that accommodates visionary and effective action especially in relations between the sexes, where so much behavior is instinctual, programmed, and seemingly outside the bounds of normative theory? Does the philosopher provide some explanation of how common unifying progressive goals can be established that are not authoritarian and that accommodate diverse aspirations? Does the philosopher provide some way of closing the apparent gap between feeling and caring on the one hand and justice and rights on the other in a way that acknowledges principle and human relation? What is the final good that should be aimed at? Where might one look for inspiration? Can it be found in the past, as Kant suggests, in a study of the Greek and Latin classics, or should other ancient sources be canvassed such as the Kabbalah?

Third, perhaps the most difficult question of all: What can we hope for? Throughout the modern period, characterized by the enormous success of mechanical explanations in science and technological applications of science, philosophers ruminated on the conflict between the deterministic material-ism assumed by modern science and the seemingly ineradicable human sense that things should be better and that with human effort they can become better. As the drive to eliminate any non-empirical "metaphysical" concepts and questions intensified in twentieth-century philosophy, this primal modern puzzle was shelved. Philosophy became more and more descriptive: this is the way our language works; these are the language games we happen to play; this is the logic we follow; this is the way our brains are wired. Reading as a feminist aware of the effect on women and disadvant-aged groups of ways in which "we" currently think, act, and talk, the normative element in philosophy is not so easily left behind.

Given modern science, and the "success" of the scientific view of the world, how are ideals to be realized? How should humans live? What kinds of relations should they have? How is it possible to believe that with human effort idealistic goals can be realized? Much as the disappointed and some-times misogynous Kant seems an unlikely source of inspiration, Kant's questions are also feminist questions.

Further reading

"Women's ways of knowing" are explored in Linda Alcoff and Elizabeth Potter's collection *Feminist Epistemologies*, and by Sandra Harding in *Whose Science? Whose Knowledge?* Harding also considers the effects of race on methods in science in *The "Racial" Economy of Science*. Jane Duran gives an overview of femi-nist epistemologies and their relation to mainstream analytic epistemologies in *Philosophies of Science/Feminist Theories*.

Carol Gilligan described her findings that women experience a different moral development and have a different moral voice in *In a Different Voice*. Two collections of papers with a variety of approaches to the controversy in ethics between "feminine" ethics of care and "masculine" duty ethics are Claudia Card's *Feminist Ethics* and Eve Cole and Susan McQuin's *Explorations in Feminist Ethics*. Monique Wittig's argument that "woman" is a suspect category is in *The Straight Mind*. See also Judith Butler's discussion of the revolutionary possibilities in transgressing gender in *Gender Trouble*.

The philosophical implications of Barbara McClintock's Nobel Prize winning work in genetics are described in Keller's *A Feeling for the Organism*. See also Keller's *Secrets of Life, Secrets of Death* and *Making Sense of Life*.

8

FEMINIST CRITICAL THEORY
AFTER KANT

Kant's overriding aim was critical, the launching of a powerful and passionate onslaught against dogma, polemic, and speculative theology. For Kant the scope of what can be known a priori by reason alone—namely the necessary spatial and temporal dimensions of human experience and some very general logical forms and categories necessary for objective judgment—was very small. Constantly Kant warned against the improper use of the "transcendent" and purely "regulative" supposition that there must be something beyond the world as experienced by humans in space and time. Never should the idea of "things-in-themselves" go beyond supposition; never should one think that there could be any substantive knowledge beyond experience.

Kant's "unity of apperception" provides only a small basis of commonality, uniting humans in a common spatial and temporal world. Human experience, unlike animal sensation, is never strictly private. My experiences are mine. But to be "experience" at all, to take the form of communicable impressions or ideas, experience presupposes an objective world of space and time that is a community in the sense that objects and events in that world are interconnected. Any representation involves the sense that my ideas are mine in a form that potentially can be communicated to others. If this is true, reconciliation between standpoint theory and objective truth cannot lie either in the establishment of a privileged standpoint from which to view things-in-themselves (of an underclass, oppressed races, a subordinated sex) or in the establishment of a direct link (by way of ostension or observation) between things-in-themselves and representations. For Kant, both are illusory and an improper use of metaphysics. Unexperienced reality must remain unexperienced, marking only a negative limit beyond which knowledge cannot go.

So Kant mapped out a "small Safe Island," or modest "secure dwelling house," of truth. To venture out on the high seas of extrasensory speculation about God, the soul, or purpose in the cosmos, he warned, is very danger-ous. Inherent in Kant's caution was a sense of human diversity. Given the limited materials with which human knowledge must be constructed—space, time, causality, elementary logic—any attempt at a "Tower of Babel" is doomed. A diversity of "tongues" ensures differences between builders of knowledge around the world, with the result that different groups will build knowledge after their own design (Critique of Judgment, p. 573). There can be no conquering the world in the name of truth, only the building of humble "dwelling houses" obeying the structural laws of physical reality, big enough for science and perhaps some overlooking of science on the part of a properly critical philosophy that sees that science does not go arrogantly beyond the boundaries of empirical knowledge.

For many analytic readers of philosophy the empty positing of an unknow-able world of things-in-themselves was already too much metaphysics, but for Kant the supposition of a noumenal world is the necessary source of the impulse that presses critique past "weariness and complete indifference" (Cri-tique of Pure Reason, p. 8). To go on with critical reflection once one becomes aware of the limits of knowledge assumes that thought and action are not irrevocably determined by pre-existing material causes, that there is reason to hope that human purposes can be realized, and that something comes of right action. These suppositions allow Kant's Critique of Pure Reason to end not with Humean skepticism but with the outlines of a critical practice in which reason is "disciplined," and so loses some of its dangerous tendency to dogmatism and autocracy. It is a process that Kant admitted might seem strange.

> But that reason, whose proper duty it is to prescribe a discipline for all other endeavors, should itself stand in need of such discipline may indeed seem strange; and it has, in fact, hitherto escaped this humiliation, only because, in view of its stately guise and estab-lished standing, nobody could lightly come to suspect it of idly substituting fancies for concepts, and words for things.
>
> (Critique of Pure Reason, p. 575)

Reason must discipline itself, said Kant. Especially it must do so when reason takes the form of a "culture" that develops around a set of skills or behaviors that tries in the name of reason to barricade itself against critique (p. 575). As examples of the need for discipline, Kant singled out quasi-geometric or logical versions of philosophy that propose to begin with rigid definitions and axioms and proceed to demonstrations of truth. Such philosophies are no more than "houses of cards" or "empty air," said Kant (p. 585). Definitions, unless of arbitrarily invented words, are never complete or clear but always limited. They vary among individuals and are explanatory, expository, and open to revision. As a consequence, demonstrations are only as valid as the uncertain concepts in which their premises are expressed. Only in mathematics can there be axioms and proofs.

Equally in need of critique, said Kant, is "polemical" response to undisciplined reason. Polemical attacks—Marxist, humanist, atheist, feminist—on a dogmatic or established culture or set of beliefs assume dogmatic positions of their own from which to attack, and these positions are therefore as much in need of "discipline" as the dogmas of their opponents. Somehow the discipliner of reason must criticize without herself becoming a dogmatist or polemicist. Here, one feminist reader of Kant pointed out, is the paradox of any critical theory, including feminist critical theory (Kimberly Hutchings in *Kant, Critique, and Politics*). Critique constantly undermines its own critical stance. To be critical requires a principle or value on which to base criticism. If a position is to be claimed wrong, it must be wrong in the name of some truth. But if the critic assumes such a truth, she has become a dogmatist herself. On what can feminists base a critique of philosophy or culture if not on the idea of a feminine essence, or the privilege of a woman's standpoint? Criticism, including feminist criticism, requires a perpetual oscillation between authoritarianism and relativism, between the assumption of necessary truth and the denial of any truth at all. Even when feminists follow Foucault and propose a contrarian perpetual critique disruptive of any "regime of truth," said Hutchings, even then they assume dogmatically the uncriticized value of freedom and self-creation. Nor did Hutchings find Kant's own account of the dogma-free disciplining of reason convincing.

A successful critic, as described by Kant in the concluding chapters of the *Critique of Pure Reason*, takes neither the dogmatic nor the polemic position. He (or she) remains on the sideline as onlooker, "from the safe seat of the critic" (p. 598). Eventually the argument dies down, "opposing parties having learned to recognize the illusions and prejudices which have set them at variance" (p. 599). Such a removed disinterested stance alone might seem no better than Humean skepticism and of little use to a committed reformer.

But, said Kant, the critic can go a step further. Beyond amusement, skepticism, and indifference, he, or she, can move to surer ground, immune to the charge of dogmatism. Heated irresolvable conflicts—conflicts between standpoint and empiricist epistemologies, between essentialism and social constructivism, between determinism and visionary politics, for example—may have no "practical outcome" by themselves, but if debate is carried out freely, sincerely, and with thoroughness, it can advance understanding and with it reconciliation. In time, as long as the critic is not drawn into debate as dogmatist or polemicist, an antinomy will appear at the core of the dispute, revealing a boundary beyond which reason cannot go. At this point the "limits of reason" are known with absolute certainty. Critical reason has become a non-dogmatic "tribunal" that gives the "peace of a legal order," legislating limits to dispute and putting to rest controversy (p. 601). By showing the futility of debate about what one cannot know, critical reason sets—not customary or habitual limits as with Hume—but necessary limits to knowledge. It can do so with certainty because reason is in a privileged position in respect to itself. This, said Kant, makes his critical method more powerful than Hume's. Hume's critique lacks force, is based on conjecture, and is easily refuted. But once the necessary limits of reason are understood, the craving that pushes a thinker out on the wild uncharted seas of speculation is both curbed and satisfied. He knows something with certainty, even if it is only a boundary beyond which he cannot go.

It is not surprising that feminist critical theorists, pressed by more than metaphysical cravings, are likely to require more from critical theory than the end of hostilities, but some feminist readers of Kant found hints of further emancipatory possibilities in critical method described in the concluding passages of the Critique of Pure Reason. Kant, they said, veered from a legislative and possibly authoritative dogmatic function of critical reason to procedural considerations that promise more than cessation of debate. Understanding the limits of reason, said Kant, establishes the "right to submit openly for discussion the thoughts and doubts with which we find ourselves unable to deal and to do so without being decried as troublesome and dangerous citizens" (Critique of Pure Reason, p. 602). For women whose contributions had been dismissed or excluded, this alone was a welcome principle, but Kant's non-dogmatic and non-polemic critical stance does more than allow the expression of differing viewpoints. In open and sincere discussion, a disputant may work toward a shared and sympathetic grasp of the roots of a conflict as understood by both sides. As Kant put it, she "develops the dialectic which lies concealed in [her] own breast no less than in that of [her] antagonist" (p. 603). Resisting being drawn into an exchange of sophistic arguments invented to support opposing theses, the critic achieves a deeper understanding of controversy. Feminist philosophers often expressed discomfort with the hostile and fruitless adversarial style of philosophical discussion. Here, in a few brief passages, Kant seemed to project not only tolerance but a more participatory and constructive style of debate.

Following the thread of these ideas as they were taken up and developed in post-Kantian German critical theory, feminist critical theorist Seyla Benhabib addressed the paradox—how is critical practice possible if it assumes neither a dogmatic norm nor a visionary utopia (Critique, Norm, and Utopia)? Firmly rejecting postmodern approaches that embrace relativism, she found the beginnings of a feminist critical practice and emancipatory politics in Jurgen Habermas's *Theory of Communicative Action*. Habermas suffered from a limited masculine perspective, said Benhabib; he could, for example, call marriage "heaven in a heartless world," a characterization that would make little sense to a woman. But this defect can be diagnosed and corrected. A deeper problem lies in the excessive formalism of the procedural principles that are Habermas's version of Kant's discipline of reason. Starting from Kant's brief suggestions of a discursive ethics, Habermas articulated norms for discussion regulated by principles to which everyone can conform as rational beings. The derivation of such universally acceptable rules involves understanding others, but others for Habermas are not concrete others—women, people of color, workers—but a "generalized other." Too often, said Benhabib, that other is, just like Habermas himself, a white European male academic. As a result, the normative rules that are to guarantee a truthful outcome do not reflect the fact of difference, the fact of unique needs, talents, and capacities. In addition to the rules of order of public discourse, suggested Benhabib, some consideration is needed of affective bonds between people who are different, bonds like friendship, solidarity, and loyalty. Habermas was led astray by Kant and by the philosophical tradition. He reasserted the rule of reason over feeling. He relegated affective relations to ineffective aesthetic and expressive activities (Critique, Norm, and Utopia, pp. 340–1). The weakness, said Benhabib, can be overcome by an infusion of feminist ethics and a closer reading of Kant.

On the one hand are formal rules of procedure where everyone is equal, but within which nothing substantive can be decided. On the other hand are particular self-interests and loyalties of different groups. Again antinomy resurfaces between dogmatism and relativism. In order to articulate a nexus between individual self-interest and universal principles that avoids the "either relativism or dogmatism paradox," Benhabib turned to Hannah Arendt, another innovative reader of Kant. When tradition has utterly failed, as Arendt believed it had in the twentieth century, how can one dare to act? On what principle? Arendt's major concern was with the Holocaust, environmental collapse, and nuclear war, but the question can also be asked in feminist terms. Given that the Western tradition has been dominated by men, given that its physical and theoretical constitution has been based on racial and sexual inequality, how is feminist action possible? How can a woman have any sense of what to do? How can she have any sense of what she can know, what she might accomplish, and what she might hope for? How can she dare to take action, given the tragic outcome, as Kant himself noted, of so many idealistic schemes?

Arendt found inspiration in Kant for answers to these kinds of questions. If together in a public arena of political action, free citizens sincerely present their stories and ideas to each other and are heard by others, out of that process might come principles that can be the basis for political action. The danger that projects will miscarry is tempered by the assurance that actions will be judged in "public" tolerant discussion, by a free press and a free academy. Political action will be restrained and, in the case of failure, forgiven so new beginnings can be made.

Putting together Arendt's Kant, the post-Kantian discourse theory of Jurgen Habermas, and feminist ethics that emphasize feeling for and relationships with "concrete" others, Benhabib theorized a feminist critical practice that was to steer between the authoritarian dangers of transcendent principle and the nihilism of postmodern relativism. From Habermas she took an extensive elaboration of Kant's call for freedom of speech as necessary normative condition for participatory debate. She supplemented what otherwise might have been a purely formal abstraction with insights into relations between self and other taken from feminist ethics. She added Arendt's interpretation of Kantian judgment as a mediating device by which transcendent truth is replaced by thought and judgment from the perspective of concrete others whom one knows. Political participants would no longer read, think, or judge only as a woman, or even as a feminist, but as a man, child, African, domestic worker, as every man and every woman.

The post-Kantian ethical constructions of Onora O'Neill draw on some of the same sources. Kant's categorical imperative and maxim that people should be treated as ends and not means, said O'Neill, can be humanized and relativized for particular circumstances of interest to women, such as coercion and deception in prostitution and pornography, respect and abuse in sexual relationships, and the treatment of children. Again the key to correct moral and legal judgment is public discussion that establishes norms and policies with general and not just particular validity.

O'Neill expanded on Kant's call for "tolerance" in the concluding chapters of the *Critique of Pure Reason* (*Constructions of Reason*, pp. 28–50). What Kant meant or should have meant, she said, is not freedom of speech as it is usually understood in liberal democracies. If speech is allowed but elicits only indifference, if it is not heard or understood, then nothing is accomplished. Tolerated speech, said O'Neill is public speech that elicits response. Speech tailored for a particular audience, or group of supporters, relying on an accepted bedrock of common assumptions such as that God exists, or that women are oppressed, or that a workers' state is the only free state, or that evolution is necessary truth, is not spoken to be heard and understood by everyone. Kantian toleration, said O'Neill, is double-pronged, imposing obligations on hearers and speakers alike. To speak "publicly" in Kant's sense is to be willing to call any assumption into question, to depend on no unexamined consensus.

In order to explain how agreement among diverse people is possible, O'Neill and Benhabib, like Arendt, turned from Kant's remarks on the disciplining of reason in the *Critique of Pure Reason* to the first part of the *Critique of Judgment* on aesthetic judgment. There Kant had made passing reference to a "sensus communis." This he distinguished both from ordinary common sense, which is only compacted social prejudice, and from the necessary shared logic of objective judgments of fact. "In all judgments by which we describe anything as beautiful," said Kant, "we allow no one to be of another opinion, without, however, grounding our judgments on concepts but only on our feelings, which we therefore place at its basis, not as a private, but as a common feeling" (*Critique of Judgment*, p. 76). Creatively expanding this brief mention of the presumption of a "common feeling" in aesthetic judgment, feminist critical theorists worked to deflect and adapt the Kantian legacy. Arendt's, Benhabib's, and O'Neill's Kant moved away from alienated emotionless reason. He began to develop the idea of an integrated human being capable of both rational and feeling response. He projected the ability to synthesize one's own sensations with the needs and desires of others.

Kant had often been accused by feminists of denying the role of emotion in knowledge and morality; now a careful reading of the *Critique of Judgment* indicated that it was not all feeling that Kant excluded but only certain kinds of feeling. Within the vague category of "emotion," defined only negatively as what is not rational, Kant made distinctions. Both humans and animals have instinctive drives for nutrition and sex. Although Kant credits these drives with considerable importance in maintaining health and in providing pleasurable recreation, they do not figure in knowledge or morality. More dangerous to morality are sophisticated human desires for objects that bring future pleasures, either sensual pleasures or pleasure in being famous or exercising power. Antithetical to both knowledge and morality are stronger "agitations," such as obsessive and unhealthy hatred, rage, or love.

But Kant also described other more benign kinds of feeling response. He cited feelings of respect and loving admiration that can attach to the contemplation of a moral principle, to principled moral action, or to a virtuous person. He alluded to the pleasure a researcher takes in the discovery of principles that unite several different phenomena. Most important for feminist critical theorists, Kant described a pleasurable sense of beauty that is not the same as, but analogous and interactive with moral pleasure (*Critique of Judgment*, p. 23). Here at the very level of direct intuitive sensibility, unmediated by logic or mathematical grids of space and time, the judgment that a thing is beautiful, said Kant, presupposes a shared and enlarged response that is presumed to be common to all.

Aesthetics has its own modern history. Cartesian attempts to find rational principles that account for beauty gave way to Hume's empirical derivation of standards of taste. Descriptive accounts of the mechanisms of perception were replaced by the Third Earl of Shaftesbury's romantic spiritualist celebration of form in nature. In Germany Baumgarten expanded the concept of aesthetics from fine art to perceptual response in general. Kant followed Shaftesbury and Baumgarten's lead. As with Shaftesbury and Baumgarten, aesthetic reaction for him was a universal and perpetual response of human beings to beauty in nature and to imitations of nature in decorative arts. Shells, bird wings, flowers, landscapes, and also gardens, wall papers, table decorations, furniture designs, fabrics with motifs borrowed from nature, all were used by Kant as examples of the beauty of form which gives aesthetic pleasure, presumably pleasure shared by all.

In fine art, said Kant, aesthetic judgment is less certain and less common. Although development of a social consensus in aesthetics is a natural development given the communicability inherent in aesthetic judgment, in art the fact of agreement can become more important than any real feeling response to beauty. As a result, all sorts of social and commercial interests intercede. Art connoisseurs are often given up to "idle, capricious, mischievous passions" (Critique of Judgment, p. 140). Although the appreciation of beauty in nature is a sign of a good soul, this may not be true in the case of exhibitors and patrons of art. Kant's aesthetic sensibility is not the exclusive province of Hume's sophisticated experienced European museum goer. It is shared by native peoples, expressed universally in gardens, fashions, body paint, home decorating. It is a response to bird songs, flowers, seashells, ice crystals, in which aspects of nature stripped away by mechanical science are rediscovered.

Again the challenge as Kant saw it is the negotiation of antinomy, the steering between two seemingly necessary, but contradictory and also intolerable alternatives. The judgment that a thing is beautiful seems necessarily to be a statement of personal response—"This gives me pleasure." Alternatively, the fact that we argue about beauty indicates that there is a fact of the matter, and some set of criteria determines the thing-in-itself that is beauty. Two apparently inescapable alternatives are both unacceptable on theoretical and pragmatic grounds. A personal statement is inconsistent with the logic of beauty judgments. Beauty can be argued and debated, which would make no sense if aesthetic appreciation is a private sensation of pleasure. Alternatively, there seems to be no way to define beauty rationally as one might give an account of a natural phenomenon in science, given the great variety of forms of beauty and the emotional nature of responses to beauty. In the first case, there is little point to sharing beauty; each person remains locked in his own private sensations. In the second, a dogmatic standard illegitimately imposes an arbitrary standard, making beauty calculable from some fixed set of criteria.

In this conflict in Kantian aesthetics, between personal response and universal judgment, feminist theorists saw a possible political analogy. In politics the dilemma is similar. Political judgment either assumes an unwarranted dogmatic universality or is an expression of individual feeling without applicability to others. Could the communicability tentatively imagined by Kant as inherent in judgments of beauty be used as a bridge between individual or group self-interest and universal judgment so as to generate political principles common to all? Kant's aesthetic sensibility to beauty directly incorporates human sociability in that it involves a projected sense of

135

how others will respond. Alone on a desert island, not many, said Kant, would decorate their huts or persons. The sense of beauty is a communal sense, not in the sense of being programmed or caused either genetically or socially, but in the sense we have of living together in a world in which form and structure reflect human ideals. An individual forming an aesthetic judgment knows that she judges for concrete different others as well as for herself, and is ready to face those others' responses in free tolerant discussion. If such a judgment is used as a prototype not just in aesthetics but also for political judgment, the feminist critic might be able to balance on the edge of Hutching's paradox, not judging only from her own perspective, and not imposing on others a dogmatic or polemical principle.

The suggestions in the *Critique of Judgment* of communicability and common sensibility are not developed at any length. Kant provided no theory of power, no way of thinking about material and political barriers to participation in scientific, political, or aesthetic debates. He gave no account of the ways in which self-interest and bias infect judgment, and so provided no critical procedure for uncovering metaphors and constructs that distort findings in science, such as have been exposed by feminist epistemologists. Like other modern philosophers, he neglected language and the role played by language structures in shaping concepts and inferences. Nevertheless, Kant provided for feminists the germ of an idea by which paradoxes in critical theory might be reconciled.

Kant might also offer ways to approach feminist antinomies. How is it possible to steer a course between relativism and confidence in science as usual? A critical feminist theorist after Kant would not give up objectivity. She would not give up the regulative transcendence of assuming that there is a truth to be approached, causal mechanisms to be sought, and a global "community" to the physical world in which events are interactive. She would diligently work for consistency in scientific theory. At the same time she would not assume that a direct correspondence could be established between theories and things-in-themselves. She would remain open to resynthesization of her and other's experience. Given the importance of intuitive and aesthetic attention to form and purpose in nature, hers would be a science open to different styles of research. It would be a science that provides public forums in which speech is "tolerant" in O'Neill's Kantian sense. The result would be a successive enlargement of scientific knowledge, and avoidance of blind spots and distortions as were encountered in genetics by Keller and McClintock.

FEMINIST CRITICAL THEORY AFTER KANT

Functional form exists in nature in two ways for Kant, first as a necessary presupposition in biological research, as was also pointed out by Keller, and second as the basis for the communicability of beauty in nature. Following Kant's lead in the *Critique of Judgment*, mechanisms, including mechanisms that causally determine masculine and feminine behavior, can and should be studied in evolutionary biology and genetics, but they could be studied with the understanding that ideas of form and function play a formative role, not as unwarranted assumptions or imported metaphors but as the result of direct aesthetic appreciation of perceived reality. Science in this sense is not a tabulation of prerecorded research results that assumes an unexamined infrastructure of concepts, but requires direct perceptual intuition and attentiveness to natural processes and structures such as Keller found in the work of McClintock. Biological structures and processes play a role in survival and reproduction; organic form gives aesthetic pleasure, a necessary aspect of scientific investigation.

Related is a possible resolution to debates surrounding essentialism. Following Kant, femininity or masculinity might be retained as substantive ideals. On this view, femininity would not be a thing-in-itself, a natural straitjacket or pre-existing form to which all women must and should conform. Nor would femininity be a genetic mechanism that is necessarily adaptive and successful given the logic of neo-Darwinian evolutionary theory. Femininity, as well as masculinity or humanity, might be taken as a quasi-aesthetic functional ideal, open to the enlargement that comes from seeing women and men from and for many perspectives. A moral theorist, then, unless she or he restricts the scope of philosophy to description of existing uses of moral language or existing moral behavior, might evoke a communicable ideal of a virtuous and therefore beautiful man, woman, or human. Without assuming a fixed biological purpose, or a purely private response, aesthetic judgment links that ideal with others. Judgments on current standards and norms of femininity or masculinity are made for others, and so are judgments that can and must be debated freely, sincerely, and publicly. On this view, femininity, masculinity, humanity, are not provable statistics, nor are they projections of personal feeling, but the result of judgment that must be enlarged by communication and mutual understanding. Nowhere is this clearer than in Kant's distinction between potentially universal human ideals and human norms that vary by race and location. "A Negro," said Kant, "must have a different idea of the beauty of the [human figure] from a white man, a Chinaman a different normal idea from a European" (*Critique of Judgment*,

p. 71). Ideal beauty, said Kant, is different. It "consists in the expression of the moral without which the object would not please universally" (p. 72).

Neither Kant nor post-Kantian critical feminist theorists have yet given a very clear account of how such public tolerated speech and enlarged judgment is to be fostered. Sometimes Kant seems content to be an elitist, assuming that masses of people will remain at the level of animal sensation and will take the word of the educated classes as to what is beautiful and moral. Other times, still with a note of condescension, Kant suggests that less tutored and more natural responses such as those of non-European peoples and lower classes are needed to temper elitist sensibility in order to create a "true" aesthetic culture. Such a culture, he projected, must be based on "the art of reciprocal communication of ideas between the cultivated and uncultivated classes," a communication that will "harmonize the large-mindedness and refinement of the former with the natural simplicity and originality of the latter" (Critique of Judgment, p. 201). Given that neither elitism nor a token injection of "enriching" diversity is likely to satisfy feminist critics, more would have to be said about a truly cosmopolitan aesthetic culture. Material arrangements would have to be designed to ensure that the voices of working people, of postcolonial people, of women, are heard and understood. Some account is necessary of mechanisms that could force the installation of those arrangements, given that those in power have an interest in silencing others.

Most speculative, and most suspect from a contemporary point of view, are Kant's perilous ventures on the stormy seas of metaphysical speculation about freedom of the will. At this point, given the current antimetaphysical climate in philosophy, all but the most foolhardy of feminist philosophers might turn back, especially as one virtue often claimed by feminist philosophy is a grounding in practice that protects against empty theorizing. Deduction without content and logical systems without reference have to be less tempting for feminists always called back to the reality of women's condition and women's aspirations. But the Kantian line of critical thought leads directly from the antinomy between determinism and practical efficacy of purpose to cosmic questions of meaning. By Kant's reasoning, the moral beauty or political purpose that is the object of a "sensus communis" presupposes a moral purpose to human life and in turn moral purpose in the cosmos. Without that perilous venture into metaphysics, Kant's "sense in common" is in danger of becoming either groundless presumption that allows a feminist critic to impose her view on others, or standardless coherence to feminist correctness.

Paradoxically, it is the very practical and pragmatic impulse of feminist philosophy, a pragmatism shared with Kant, that creates the necessity for speculation about cosmic purpose and design in nature. Without that pragmatic purpose, current analytic paradigms such as naturalized epistemology and scientific realism can avoid metaphysics, restricting philosophizing to accounts that are "descriptive" and critical only of other philosophers. Future feminists who ask not just "What can I know?" but also "What can I hope for?" may be obliged to set sail on Kant's uncharted seas, guided only by his last tentative hint of a possible synthesis of aesthetic sensibility, science, and a human kingdom of ends.

Further reading

Seyla Benhabib elaborates on debates surrounding Habermas's discourse theory in *The Communicative Ethics Controversy*. For Arendt's reading of Kant see her *Lectures on Kant's Political Philosophy*. For an overview of Arendt's adaptation of Kantian critique see in addition to Hutching's *Kant, Critique, and Politics*, the chapters on Arendt in Nye, *Philosophia*.

AFTERWORD
The weight of the past

In her book *The Life of the Mind* Hannah Arendt retold a parable from Kafka. The present, she said, is a struggle to find breathing space and a foothold while fighting back two adversaries. One is the past that presses us forward at all costs. The other is the future, facing us as we turn away from the past, and equally menacing. Wearied by an exhausting and fruitless struggle against past and future, Kafka's protagonist has a dream. He dreams that he jumps out of the fighting line, out of time and history to a place away from the fray. From there he looks down on his old adversaries, the past and the future, as they fight it out with each other.

The situation of feminist philosophers is not so different. On the one hand the weight of the Western intellectual tradition can seem overwhelming. Solidly masculine, structured around a sex/gender system, expressing men's politics and men's interests, it presses a woman philosopher forward. Kant's and Rousseau's overt misogyny, Hume's patronizing condescension, Locke's defense of slavery, an almost universal presumption of European superiority, all force a woman philosopher to look to the future. But the future can be equally threatening. The feminization of poverty, fundamentalist religious movements, mass weapons in the hands of terrorists, and increasing signs of environmental collapse all force the woman philosopher back to face the past. Postmodern and deconstructive perspectives can make the prospect worse. With no standards of reason, no rules of morality, no principles, no tradition to prevent anarchy and dissolution of the social fabric, with only rampant relativism and diversity that might include fascism, extremism, sadism, or nihilism, what hope is there for the future? And so the woman philosopher turns back again to challenge and accuse the past.

Arendt pointed to the extraordinary nature of this particular present moment in time. Ordinarily tradition carries life continuously on without much of a fight. Buffeted by occasional accidents and inevitable turning points, women and men live in a flow of communal understanding, habit, and custom. In exceptional times, like the present, when tradition breaks down, the enervating and destructive fighting off of both past and future becomes necessary. The Holocaust, acts of unimaginable terrorist violence, unremitting assaults on women and children make idealistic thought about human nature quixotic. Traditional religious belief is increasingly anomalous given modern science. Gender and ethnic studies document oppressive caste systems in virtually all human societies. It is no wonder that a woman philosopher might be tempted to dream Kafka's escape from real time, that she might try to find refuge in visionary separatist communities of the future or mythical matriarchies of the distant past. Certainly Western philosophy as it stands can seem an implacable antagonist, a solid phalanx of theories, philosophies, disciplines, and institutions to which women have not contributed and that are prejudicial to women's interests. But, said Arendt, there is another possibility, one that might give an embattled thinker a foothold in the present and prevent her from being crushed to extinction between past and future. There might be a diagonal line of thought and action that turns the future in new directions. The key to such deflection, she believed, is in the past, the philosophical past that is our present heritage.

As the various approaches to history considered here indicate, there is no one way to confront the past. History can be canvassed for purposes of detection and indictment of unacceptable attitudes and beliefs. Feminists have searched for and found sexism and racism in many of the canonical texts of modern philosophy. Challenged to show why the sexism or racism of a thinker is relevant to theories of ethics or knowledge, feminist critics have gone deeper to show how discriminatory attitudes shape superficially generic concepts, arguments, and conclusions. In this process of uncovering the relation between sexist or racist attitudes and general philosophical claims, a subtle change in feminist approach can occur. If the original impulse was hostile, exposing the experiential sources of philosophy brings richer and deeper understanding. A historian, who began by positioning herself dogmatically as the enemy of philosophy, may find threads of possible common cause. A historian who began with standard versions of philosophical positions can come to see networks of ideas with deep roots in human experience. Feminist readings of Kant are a case in point. The textbook Kant may seem an egregious wrong-thinker. Attention, however, to his modernist antinomies and critical theory subtly deflects Kantian philosophy in new, more positive directions.

Initially the feminist historian in opposition to philosophy has much in common with the analytic reader of philosophy who, also from a dogmatic present position, interprets past philosophers in his own contemporary terms and looks for error and validity according to his own standards. A feminist historian might begin with a sure sense of sexist attitudes and beliefs harmful to women and search for them in philosophical texts. After that there is a difference. The analytic critic's logic rules out both history and future development; his logic remains invariable. When attitudes and beliefs are placed in historical and experiential context, however, the feminist reader's sense of direction can begin to shift. She may begin thinking "with" a philosopher, or "after" a philosopher, or through tensions in a philosopher's thought, both combating and allying herself with tradition as in Arendt's neo-Kantian studies, or Weil's revisionary Cartesianism.

Neither Arendt nor Weil accepted the past at face value. Neither uncritically accepted either contemporary or contemporaneous interpretations of past philosophers. Weil rejected the view of Descartes as a prototypical rationalist and projected an alternative practicalist direction for contemporary epistemology. Arendt worked with Kant through modernist dilemmas to some hope for future protection against evils like the Holocaust. Although it can seem in such studies that feminist convictions have been laid aside in rapprochement with the "enemy," complicity with tradition creates possibilities for the future. Feminist readings of philosophy focused on finding new directions for modernist philosophy rather than on the blanket indictment of modernism leave open the possibility of a future with vitalizing roots in intellectual history.

The past can be canvassed for friends instead of enemies. These might be well-known philosophers interpreted in new ways or lesser-known philosophers whose work has been neglected. These might be women like Anne Conway whose work was unappreciated in her time. Here again, as a feminist confronts the past, her sense of future direction can shift. She might begin with a set of philosophical convictions and look for matching convictions in the past. Liberal feminists, for example, approve Locke's defense of equality and freedom. Socialist feminists cite Marx on the economic causes of women's lack of power. But in the process of a close reading of supposed friendly sources, a feminist can find her beliefs developing in new directions. As Okin pointed out, when interpreted in the context of past and present political social reality, neither Locke's abstract rights nor Marx's workers' democracy may be extendable to women or minority groups, an insight that opens up new directions in political thinking.

The question that inevitably arises for both the oppositional and the friendly approach to history is: Why bother at all? If acceptable theory is currently available, finding allies or enemies in the past should not be necessary. One should simply leave history behind and continue theorizing. But theory cannot move forward in a vacuum. If it is to be more than continued artificial articulation, if it is to have vitality and momentum, it needs both a foothold in the present and a tradition out of which to develop. It is here that the Western intellectual history that officially excludes the thought of women and men of color has been so challenging. If, however, that past can be made to change, so might what passes for the "great" and guiding thoughts of modern times.

That the past might change seems a ludicrous possibility on modernist principles. Newtonian time is a series of moments, past, present, and future, lined up and ready to be known. This is the past ready to attack and defeat with all its weight the woman or man not privileged to be in the mainstream of thought. This is the future, stretching endlessly and predictably ahead, ready to cut off any escape from the past. But in real present time, where we all in fact are, the past is not fixed any more than is the future. Even if it is possible to say that at some past moment of time all the atoms that made up the world were in a particular given configuration—a hypothesis itself doubtful given twentieth-century physics—it tells us nothing about the historical past. Historical events are events with meaning, meaning never finally contained or finished but dependent on unfolding events and on subsequent interpretations. In this sense it is impossible to know what modernism was until we see what it is and will be. A choice between understanding past philosophy as if it was written in the present and understanding past philosophy as it was understood in its own historical context is often used to divide the field of historical studies. Both choices are illusory. There is no present moment sequestered from what people thought in the past. There is no past moment in which beliefs and standards different from our own were fixed and determinant.

Is this to fall back into relativism? To fall victim again to the paradox of critical theory? Is it to say that there are many readings of the past, that there is no objectivity in history any more than there is in any other field of knowledge? Hopefully not. By relating to historical texts and events in new ways, by putting texts into interaction with present concerns, by responding and thinking about what happened in the past from a present moment in time, by beginning to act and think in new ways as a result, the past of modern philosophy can be made to change. Ideas have no hard edges; they spread out in time. What they are is incorporated in chains of responses and understandings that stretch backward into the past and forward into the future. What did modernism initiate in the seventeenth century? A mechanical method that churns out techniques with no regard for the moral effects of those techniques? Or a strongly objective science in the spirit of feminist philosophers of science like Keller or McClintock? What was this Western culture? A closed canon of doctrines rooted in privileges of sex, race, and culture? Or a hybrid cosmopolitan culture where goods and ideas circulate beyond rigid lines of caste, national advantage, or corporate profit? What is the legacy of Cartesianism? Is it the legacy of a rational scientific method divorced from intuition, feeling, and moral consequences, the legacy of a dualism of atomic mechanisms and directing disembodied minds? Or is it Weil's practical worker's science and Elisabeth's morally responsible medical practice?

Philosophers have always fought with the past. They have used powerful weapons, weapons like logical refutation, hostile counter-examples, and on occasion dismissive parody. Feminists approaching history tend to use less lethal but no less effective tools of understanding, amplification, and explication, tools designed not so much to destroy as to disarm and deflect. In the process, feminists discover a modern philosophy that may not be the same as we thought it was, with a future not quite as we imagined it would be. Modern philosophy was, and may be in the future, a liberal art addressing the deep intellectual tensions in modern life, rather than an academic specialty allied with linguistics and cognitive psychology. Philosophy was, and may be, a community of thinkers at odds with university teaching that is protective of existing methods and vested interests. Modern philosophy was, and may be, open to a variety of insights from cultural and ethnic studies, literature, developments in science, and the perspectives of skilled workers and technicians. Philosophy was, and may be, conducted in open forums so that many different voices speaking and writing in many styles are heard and tolerated. Modern philosophy was, and may be, a collaborative rather than an adversarial endeavor carried on between fellow thinkers instead of embittered rivals.

BIBLIOGRAPHY OF WORKS CITED

Alcoff, Linda and Potter, Elizabeth (eds) (1993) *Feminist Epistemologies*, New York: Routledge.

Anthony, Louise and Witt, Charlotte (eds) (1993) *A Mind of One's Own: Feminist Essays on Reason and Objectivity*, Boulder, CO: Westview Press.

Appleby, Joyce, Hunt, Lynn, and Jacob, Margaret (eds) (1994) *Telling the Truth about History*, New York: W. W. Norton.

Arendt, Hannah (1978) *The Life of the Mind*, New York: Harcourt Brace Jovanovich.

—— (1954) *Between Past and Future*, London: Faber and Faber.

—— (1954) *Lectures on Kant's Political Philosophy*, Chicago: University of Chicago Press.

Arneil, Barbara (1996) *John Locke and America*, Oxford: Clarendon Press.

Baier, Annette (1985) *Postures of the Mind: Essays on Mind and Morals*, Minneapolis: University of Minnesota Press.

—— (1997) *A Progress of Sentiments: Reflections on Hume's Treatise*, Cambridge, MA: Harvard University Press.

—— (1997) *The Commons of the Mind*, La Salle, IL: Open Court.

Bar On, Bat-Ami (ed.) (1994) *Modern Engendering: Critical Feminist Readings in Modern Western Philosophy*, Albany: State University of New York Press.

Bartky, Sandra (1990) *Femininity and Domination: Studies in the Phenomenology of Oppression*, New York: Routledge.

Bender, John and Wellberg, David (eds) (1991) *Chronotypes: The Construction of Time*, Stanford, CA: Stanford University Press.

Benhabib, Seyla (1986) *Critique, Norm and Utopia: A Study of the Foundations of Critical Theory*, New York: Columbia University Press.

—— (1990) *The Communicative Ethics Controversy*, Cambridge, MA: MIT Press.

Bordo, Susan (1987) *The Flight to Objectivity: Essays on Cartesianism and Culture*, Albany: State University of New York Press.

Butler, Judith (1990) *Gender Trouble: Feminism and the Subversion of Identity*, New York: Routledge.

Card, Claudia (ed.) (1991) *Feminist Ethics*, Lawrence: University Press of Kansas.

Cole, Eve Browning and McQuin, Susan Coultrop (eds) (1992) *Explorations in Feminist Ethics: Theory and Practice*, Bloomington: Indiana University Press.

Conway, Anne (1930) *The Conway Letters: The Correspondence of Anne Viscountess Conway, Henry*

More and Their Friends, 1642–1648, edited by Marjorie Hope Nicolson, New Haven, CT: Yale University Press.

—— (1982) *The Principles of the Most Ancient and Modern Philosophy,* edited by Peter Loptson, The Hague: Martinus Nijhoff.

—— (1996) *The Principles of the Most Ancient and Modern Philosophy,* edited by Allison Coudert and Taylor Corse, Cambridge: Cambridge University Press.

Coudert, Allison (1990) *The Impact of the Kabbalah in the Seventeenth Century,* London: Blackwell.

—— (1995) *Leibniz and the Kabbalah,* Dordrecht: Kluwer.

Descartes, René (1970) *Rules for the Direction of the Mind, Principles of Philosophy, Meditations on First Philosophy, Discourse on Method, Passions of the Soul,* in *The Philosophical Works of Descartes,* translated by E. S. Haldane and G. R. T. Ross, Cambridge: Cambridge University Press.

Diamond, Irene and Quinby, Lee (eds) (1988) *Feminism and Foucault: Reflections on Resistance,* Boston, MA: Northeastern University Press.

Di Stefano, Christine (1991) *Configurations of Masculinity: A Feminist Perspective on Modern Political Theory,* Ithaca, NY: Cornell University Press.

Dudley, Edward and Novak, Maximillian (eds) (1972) *The Wild Man Within: An Image in Western Thought from the Renaissance to Romanticism,* Pittsburg, PA: University of Pittsburg Press.

Duran, Jane (1998) *Philosophies of Science/Feminist Theories,* Boulder, CO: Westview Press.

Eisenstein, Zillah (1981) *The Radical Future of Liberal Feminism,* New York: Longman.

Elshtain, Jean Bethke (1981) *Public Man, Private Woman: Women in Social and Political Thought,* Princeton, NJ: Princeton University Press.

—— (1982) *The Family in Political Thought,* Amherst: University of Massachusetts Press.

Engels, Frederick (1972) *The Origin of the Family, Private Property, and the State,* translated by Alec West, edited by E. B. Leacock, London: Lawrence and Wishart.

Ermath, Elisabeth (1992) *Sequel to History: Postmodernism and the Crisis of Representational Time,* Princeton, NJ: Princeton University Press.

Firestone, Shulamith (1970) *The Dialectic of Sex,* New York: William Morrow.

Flax, Jane (1990) *Thinking Fragments: Psychoanalysis, Feminism, and Postmodernism in the Contemporary West,* Berkeley: University of California Press.

Foucault, Michel (1972) *The Archaeology of Knowledge,* New York: Harper.

—— (1976) *The History of Sexuality,* translated by R. Hurley, New York: Pantheon Books.

Fraser, Nancy and Bartky, Sandra (eds) (1992) *Revaluing French Feminism,* Bloomington: University of Indiana Press.

Fukuyama, F. (1992) *The End of History and the Last Man,* London: Hamish Hamilton.

Gilligan, Carol (1982) *In a Different Voice: Psychological Theory and Women's Development,* Cambridge, MA: Harvard University Press.

Habermas, Jürgen (1984) *The Theory of Communicative Action,* translated by Thomas McCarthy, Boston, MA: Beacon Press.

Harding, Sandra (ed.) (1993) *The "Racial" Economy of Science: Toward a Democratic Future,* Bloomington: Indiana University Press.

—— (1986) *The Science Question in Feminism,* Ithaca, NY: Cornell University Press.

—— (1991) *Whose Science? Whose Knowledge? Thinking from Women's Lives*, Ithaca, NY: Cornell University Press.

Harvey, Elizabeth and Okruhlik, Kathleen (eds) (1992) *Women and Reason*, Ann Arbor: University of Michigan Press.

Hekman, Susan (1996) *Feminist Interpretations of Michel Foucault*, University Park: University of Pennsylvania Press.

Hume, David (1957) *An Inquiry concerning the Principles of Morals*, edited by Charles Hendel, Indianapolis, IN: Bobbs-Merrill.

—— (1978) *A Treatise of Human Nature*, edited by L. A. Selby-Bigge, Oxford: Clarendon Press.

—— (1987) *Essays: Moral, Political, and Literary*, edited by Eugene F. Miller, Indianapolis, IN: Liberty Classics.

Hutchings, Kimberly (1996) *Kant, Critique, and Politics*, London: Routledge.

Irigaray, Luce (1974) *Speculum de l'autre femme*, Paris: Minuit.

—— (1985) *Speculum of the Other Woman*, translated by Gillian Gill, Ithaca, NY: Cornell University Press.

Jacobson, Anne Jaap (ed.) (2000) *Feminist Interpretations of David Hume*, University Park: Pennsylvania State University Press.

Kant, Immanuel (1951) *Critique of Judgment*, translated by S. H. Bernard, New York: Hafner Press.

—— (1956) *Critique of Practical Reason*, translated by Lewis White Beck, Indianapolis, IN: Bobbs-Merrill.

—— (1960) *Observations on the Feeling of the Beautiful and Sublime*, translated by John Goldthwait, Berkeley: University of California Press.

—— (1963) *Lectures on Ethics*, translated by Louis Infield, New York: Harper and Row.

—— (1963) *On History*, edited by Lewis White Beck, translated by L. Beck, R. E. Anchor, and E. L. Fackenheim, New York: Macmillan.

—— (1965) *Critique of Pure Reason*, translated by Norman Kemp Smith, New York: St. Martin's Press.

—— (1970) *Kant's Political Writings*, edited by Hans Reiss, translated by H. B. Nisbet, Cambridge: Cambridge University Press.

—— (1978) *Anthropology from a Pragmatic Point of View*, edited by Frederick Van de Pitte, translated by V. L. Dowdell, Carbondale: Southern Illinois Press.

—— (1987) *Foundations of the Metaphysics of Morals*, translated by L. W. Beck, Indianapolis, IN: Liberty Classics.

—— (1996) *Metaphysics of Morals*, translated by Mary Gregor, Cambridge: Cambridge University Press.

Keller, Evelyn Fox (1983) *A Feeling for the Organism: The life and Work of Barbara McClintock*, New York: W. H. Freeman.

—— (1985) *Reflections on Gender and Science*, New Haven, CT: Yale University Press.

—— (1992) *Secrets of Life, Secrets of Death: Essays on Language, Gender, and Science*, New York: Routledge.

—— (1995) *Refiguring Life: Metaphors of Twentieth Century Biology*, New York: Columbia University Press.

—— (2002) *Making Sense of Life: Explaining Biological Development with Models, Metaphors, and Machines*, Cambridge, MA: Harvard University Press.

Kittay, Eva and Meyers, Diana (eds) (1987) *Women and Moral Theory*, Totowa, NJ: Rowman and Littlefield.

Kofman, Sarah (1992) "Rousseau's Phallocratic Ends," translated by Mara Dukat, in Nancy Fraser and Sandra Bartky (eds), *Revaluing French Feminism*, Bloomington: University of Indiana Press, pp. 46–59.

Kuehn, Manfred (2001) *Kant*, Cambridge: Cambridge University Press.

Le Dœuff, Michèle (1989) *The Philosophical Imaginary*, translated by Colin Gordon, London: Athlone Press.

Lloyd, Genevieve (1984) *The Man of Reason*, Minneapolis: University of Minnesota Press.

—— (2000) "Feminism in History of Philosophy," in Miranda Fricker and Jennifer Hornsby (eds) *The Cambridge Companion to Feminism in Philosophy*, Cambridge, Cambridge University Press, pp. 245–63.

Locke, John (1924) *Essay concerning Human Understanding*, Oxford: Clarendon Press.

—— (1964) *Some Thoughts concerning Education*, Woodbury, NY: Barron's Educational Series.

—— (1970) *Two Treatises of Government*, edited by Peter Laslett, Cambridge: Cambridge University Press.

Lougee, Carolyn (1976) *Le Paradis des femmes*, Princeton, NJ: Princeton University Press.

MacIntyre, Alaisdair (1984) *After Virtue*, Notre Dame, IL: Notre Dame University Press.

Merchant, Carolyn (1972) *The Death of Nature*, San Francisco: Harper and Row.

Mitchell, Juliet (1973) *Women's Estate*, New York: Vintage Books.

Morgan, Lewis Henry (1963) *Ancient Society*, New York: World Publishing Company.

Mossner, Ernest (1980) *The Life of David Hume*, Oxford: Clarendon Press.

Nicholson, Linda (1986) *Gender and History: The Limits of Social Theory in the Age of the Family*, New York: Columbia University Press.

—— (1990) *Feminism/Postmodernism*, New York: Routledge.

Nye, Andrea (1994) *Philosophia: The Thought of Rosa Luxemburg, Simone Weil, and Hannah Arendt*, New York: Routledge.

—— (1999) *The Princess and the Philosopher: the Letters of Elisabeth of the Palatine to René Descartes*, Lanham, MD: Rowman and Littlefield.

Okin, Susan (1979) *Women in Western Political Thought*, Princeton, NJ: Princeton University Press.

O'Neill, Onora (1989) *Constructions of Reason: Kant's Practical Philosophy*, Cambridge: Cambridge University Press.

Pateman, Carole (1988) *The Sexual Contract*, Stanford, CA: Stanford University Press.

Rorty, Richard (1979) *Philosophy and the Mirror of Nature*, Princeton, NJ: Princeton University Press.

Rosenroth, Christian Knorr (1677–84) *Kabbala Denudata*, Salzbach: Abraham Lichtenthaleri.

—— (1968) *The Kabbalah Unveiled*, translated by S. M. Mather, New York: S. Weiser.

Rousseau, Jean Jacques (1928) *Confessions*, translated by W. C. Mallory, New York: Tudor Publishing.

—— (1968) *La Nouvelle Heloïse*, translated by J. H. McDowell, University Park: Pennsylvania State University Press.

—— (1978) *On the Social Contract*, translated by J. Masters, New York: St. Martin's Press.

—— (1979) *Emile*, translated by Allan Bloom, New York: Basic Books.

—— (1992) *Discourse on the Origins and Foundations of Inequality among Men* in *Collected Writings of Rousseau*, volume 3, translated by J. Bush, R. D. Masters, C. Kelly, and T. Marshall, Hanover, NH: University Press of New England.

Ruddick, Sara (1989) *Maternal Thinking*, Boston, MA: Beacon Press.

Russell, Bertrand (1900) *A Critical Exposition of the Philosophy of Leibniz*, Cambridge: Cambridge University Press.

Schott, Robin May (1993) *Cognition and Eros: A Critique of the Kantian Paradigm*, Boston, MA: Beacon Press.

—— (ed.) (1992) *Feminist Interpretations of Immanuel Kant*, University Park: Pennsylvania State University Press.

Shklar, Judith (1969) *Men and Citizens: A Study of Rousseau's Social and Political Thought*, Cambridge: Cambridge University Press.

Smith, Bernard (1992) *Imagining the Pacific: In the Wake of the Cook Voyages*, New Haven, CT: Yale University Press.

Smith, Hilda (1982) *Reason's Disciples: Seventeenth Century English Feminists*, Urbana: University of Illinois Press.

Spengler, Oswald (1926) *The Decline of the West*, translated by C. F. Atkinson, London: George Allen and Unwin.

Stone, Lawrence (1977) *The Family, Sex, and Marriage in England 1500–1800*, New York: Harper and Row.

Trouille, Mary Seidman (ed.) (1997) *Sexual Politics in the Enlightenment: Women Writers Read Rousseau*, Albany: State University of New York Press.

Tuana, Nancy (1992) *Woman and the History of Philosophy*, Dallas: University of Texas-at-Dallas Press.

Waithe, Mary Ellen (ed.) (1991) *Modern Women Philosophers 1600–1900*, volume 3 of *A History of Women Philosophers*, Dordrecht: Kluwer.

Weil, Simone (1973) *Oppression and Liberty*, translated by A Wills and J. Petrie, Amherst: University of Massachusetts Press.

—— (1987) *Formative Writings*, translated by D. T. McFarland and W. Van Ness, Amherst: University of Massachusetts Press.

—— (1997) *Gravity and Grace*, translated by Arthur Wills, Lincoln: University of Nebraska Press.

Wittgenstein, Ludwig (1953) *Philosophical Investigations*, translated by E. Anscombe, New York: Macmillan.

Wittig, Monique (1992) *The Straight Mind and Other Essays*, Boston, MA: Beacon Press.

Wollstonecraft, Mary (1998) *A Vindication of the Rights of Woman*, Cologne: Könemann.

Wood, Neal (1984) *John Locke and Agrarian Capitalism*, Berkeley: University of California Press.

Yates, Francis (1972) *The Rosicrucian Enlightenment*, London: Routledge and Kegan Paul.

Zerilli, Linda (1994) *Signifying Woman: Culture and Chaos in Rousseau, Burke, and Mill*, Ithaca, NY: Cornell University Press.

INDEX

aesthetics 17, 116, 133, 135–8
Africans 51, 87
analytic philosophy 38–9, 41, 81, 82, 89,
    96, 101, 111, 113–14, 127, 139–42
Anscombe, Elizabeth 101
Arendt, Hannah 3, 132, 139, 140–1, 142
Aristotle 51, 53, 71, 75, 84, 85, 119
Astell, Mary 36

Bacon, Francis 4
Bartky, Sandra 7
Benhabib, Seyla 131–2, 139
Berkeley, George viii, 66
Bloom, Alan: on *Emile* 31
Bordo, Susan 39–43, 45, 115; *Flight to
    Objectivity* 39–40
Butler, Judith 7

Carolina, colony of 48–9
Cartesianism 36, 45, 46–7, 74–6
Christianity 52, 70–2, 78–9
Conway, Anne 64–83, 84, 142
Cook, Captain James: voyages 13, 22, 86,
    98, 120
critical theory 128–32

Darwin, Charles 85
deconstruction 5, 7, 91–2
Derrida, Jacques 5, 7–8, 92
Descartes, René viii, ix, 2, 5, 8, 34–47, 48,
    64, 65, 66, 67, 70, 71, 72, 73, 102,
    106; *Discourse on Method* 35, 43; on ethics
    45–6; on logic 44; on mathematics
    43–4; *Meditations* 39, 42, 43; *Passions of the
    Soul* 46; on practical science 43, 45;
    Principles of Philosophy 43; psychological
    interpretations of 41; *Rules for the Direction
    of the Mind* 43–4; on women 35

difference 57, 59, 90–1, 128, 131, 138
domestic labor 55–6, 61–2
Dutch settlers at the Cape of Good Hope
    89–90, 91, 94, 96

Elisabeth of the Palatine 35, 45–6, 47,
    64–5, 68
empiricism 35, 48–9, 77, 81
Engels, Frederick 60–1
Enlightenment vii, 2, 4, 15, 79, 88
essentialism 118–19, 130, 137
ethics 2, 25, 29–31, 5, 99, 107, 113, 118,
    123–4, 132–3, 134, 137–8
evolution 75–7, 84–5, 121

femininity 118–20, 121–2, 137
Filmer, Robert 51–2
Firestone, Shulamith 58, 62
Flax, Jane 8
Foucault, Michel 5, 6–8, 11
free will and determinism 122–5
freedom of speech 133

Gama, Vasco da 92
Genesis 52, 72, 87–8
Gilligan, Carol 118, 126
God, concept of 70, 71–3, 77, 78
Greece vii

Habermas, Jürgen 4
Helmont, Francis Mercury van 64–6, 68,
    70, 71, 78–9
history xi, 1, 5, 37, 141; empiricism in 5, 9,
    48; gender bias in 9–10; of philosophy
    vii, ix, 1–2, 38, 141–4; postmodern
    approaches to 5–9; uses of 1, 37;
    women's 10
Hobbes, Thomas x, 66, 71, 72, 78, 80, 94, 95

Holocaust 3, 142
homosexuality 6–7
human nature viii, x, 3
Hume, David viii, 9, 13, 21–4, 27, 32, 34,
    65, 66, 86–7, 89, 90, 95, 99–110, 111,
    119, 130; on correction of error 106–8;
    Essays 21–4, 109; *Inquiry concerning the*
    Principles of Morals 23; on legitimacy of
    women's complaints 23; on marriage
    21–4; on the mind 102–4; on reason
    and belief 103–5; on women's
    education 24; on women's sexuality 24;
    as source for feminist resistance 24,
    108, 109–10; on role of philosophy
    100–1, 108–9; *Treatise of Human Nature*
    99–110, 103–6

Irigaray, Luce 8

Kabbalah 64, 69, 70, 71, 73, 76, 78–9, 82
Kant, Immanuel viii, 2, 5, 8, 27, 28–30,
    32, 34, 66, 81, 86, 94, 111–26,
    127–39; aesthetics 17–19, *Anthropology*
    12–17, 19–21; antinomies 116–19,
    122–4, 130, 131–2, 135, 136;
    categorical imperative 132–3; on
    character 14; communicability 135–6;
    on critical reason 26; *Critique of Judgment*
    120–1, 128, 133–8; *Critique of Pure Reason*
    127–130, 133; ethics 16, 17–18, 25;
    feminist critiques of 16, 111–12; as
    feminist resource 112, 124; on freedom
    13, 123; *Lectures on Ethics* 25–6;
    Observations on the Feeling of the Beautiful and
    Sublime 17–19, 26; and Maria Charlotta
    26, 32; on marriage 15, 16, 19, 26;
    Metaphysics of Morals 18; on passion
    13–14, 18, 30–1, 134; *sensus communis*
    133; on sex 18–21; on teleology
    120–1; on women 13–21, 25–6; on
    women's education 20–1; on women's
    legal status 26
Keller, Evelyn Fox 46, 81, 117, 121, 122
Khoikhois 89–90, 91, 92, 93–4, 97
kinship structures 58
knowledge 114–18; standpoint and
    empiricist views of 114–17, 124–5,
    130, 136
Kofman, Sarah 8
Koran 87
Kristeva, Julia 40

language 91–2, 102, 136
Le Dœuff, Michèle 8
Leibniz, Gottfried viii, 64–5, 66, 69, 73, 80
linguistics 7–8
Linnaeus (Linné, Carl von) 85–6, 120
Lloyd, Genevieve 36–8, 45; *Man of Reason* 38
Locke, John viii, ix, 2, 5, 48–63, 65, 66, 67,
    69, 76–7, 79, 80, 87–8, 102, 104, 119,
    142–3; and Carolina colony 50–1; *Essay*
    concerning Human Understanding 49, 59, 88;
    on general ideas 58–9; on marriage
    50–4; on natural law 49; on natural right
    50; on nature 49–52, 54; on paternal
    power 51–3; on slavery 50–1; *Treatises on*
    Government 49–53, 63, 87–8, 90, 95
logic 10, 26, 66, 91, 103, 129; genetic
    fallacy in 27, 28, 30, 44

McClintock, Barbara 117, 121, 126
man, nature of 50, 60–1, 84–6, 91, 119,
    121; as nominal essence 119
marriage 15, 16, 19, 21–4, 26, 50–4,
    55–6, 62, 63, 75, 86–7
Marxism 4, 57, 60, 90, 114, 142–3
mathematics 43–4, 103, 129
Merchant, Carolyn 79, 115; *Death of Nature* 4,
    46
metaphysical dualism 45–6, 73–5, 77–8,
    79–80
metaphysics 67, 71–81, 85, 124, 127–8,
    138
mind, concept of 77, 80, 101–5
Mitchell, Juliet 57
modernism xi, 2–8, 45
monads 73
monarchism 48–9, 51–2, 64
More, Henry 63, 65–6, 68, 69, 70, 78
Morgan, Lewis Henry 60

Native Americans 59, 60, 87–8
native peoples 4, 13, 15, 22, 23, 35, 51,
    59–60, 84–98, 99, 138
natural kinds 75–6, 84–5, 119–20, 137
naturalized epistemology 104–5
nature 14–16, 21, 49–50, 53–4, 58–9,
    81–2; state of 46, 49–50, 60–1, 63, 80,
    88, 95–6

Okin, Susan 28–29, 54–5, 61–2
O'Neill, Onora 132–3, 136
oppression 6–7

parenting 58
Pateman, Carol 56, 61–2
paternal power 51–2
philosophy: adversarial style of 45, 131;
 audience for 104–5; and biography
 27–8, 32, 34; canon formation in ix, x,
 65–9, 81–2; feminist readings of
 105–6, 113–14, 118, 120, 124–5, 144;
 and literature 5, 8, 96–7; and non-
 Western cultures x–xi, 3, 4;
 psychological interpretations of 25,
 41–2; and religion vii–viii, 2, 27, 34;
 role of 40–1, 62, 100–1, 108–9; as
 source for feminism 101, 108–10;
 teaching of 31–2, 79–80, 99; and war
 4; women in viii–x, 2–3, 5, 10–11, 12,
 36, 38, 111
positivism 66, 81
postmodernism 2, 5–9
Poulain de la Barre, François 36

Quakers 64–5, 66

rationalism 40, 43
reason and rationality viii, x, 4, 24, 27–8,
 30, 35–8, 43, 46–9, 70, 84, 101, 103,
 105, 108, 116, 127–30; disciplining of
 128–9; historical analysis of 37–8, 40,
 46, 48; and passion 105
religion 70, 78; and modern science 67;
 and problem of evil 76–7
Robinson Crusoe 94
Rosenroth, Christian Knorr 64, 71, 73, 76,
 79, 82
Rousseau, Jean Jacques viii, 2, 13, 15,
 20–1, 27, 67, 84–98; Discourses on the
 Origins of Inequality 89–94; Emile 20–1, 31,
 94; on the general will 95, 98; on
 sexuality 20–1, 25; Social Contract 96; on
 women's education 20–1, 24–5.
Ruddick, Sara: Maternal Thinking 3–4
Russell, Bertrand 66–7

science vii, 2, 3, 4, 45, 67, 70–1, 73–4, 81,
 114, 116, 117, 120–5; gender
 metaphors in 4
sexual contract 56
sexuality 13, 16, 18–21, 22, 24, 25, 29,
 30, 58, 86, 93
Shaftesbury, Earl of 48–9, 64
Shklar, Judith 96
slavery 50–1, 55
social contract 56, 60, 96–7
Spengler, Oswald 3
Spinoza, Benedictus de viii, 71, 72, 73,
 79
state of nature 49–52, 58, 59–61, 63, 88,
 95–6
subjectivity 5

teleology 120–1
textuality 5–7
thinking 102, 103, 105
time vii, 5, 8, 10, 11, 72, 140–4
transmigration of souls 76–7
travel literature 13, 17, 22, 35, 58, 59,
 76, 85, 86–7, 92–3, 94, 96, 98,
 120
Tuana, Nancy 113

Vietnam War 3, 4

Weil, Simone 42–5, 46–7, 81, 83, 142
Wittgenstein Ludwig 2, 4, 101, 102
Wollstonecraft, Mary 24–5, 26, 86
women: Descartes on 35; essential nature
 of 67–8, 84; Hume on 21–4, 100–1;
 Kant on 12–21, 25–6; in philosophy
 viii–ix, 5, 67–8; Rousseau on 13, 15,
 97; as signifier 91
World War II 3

Yates, Francis 79, 83

Zerilli, Linda 90–1